Beach Mindfulness

A Serene Coloring Experience

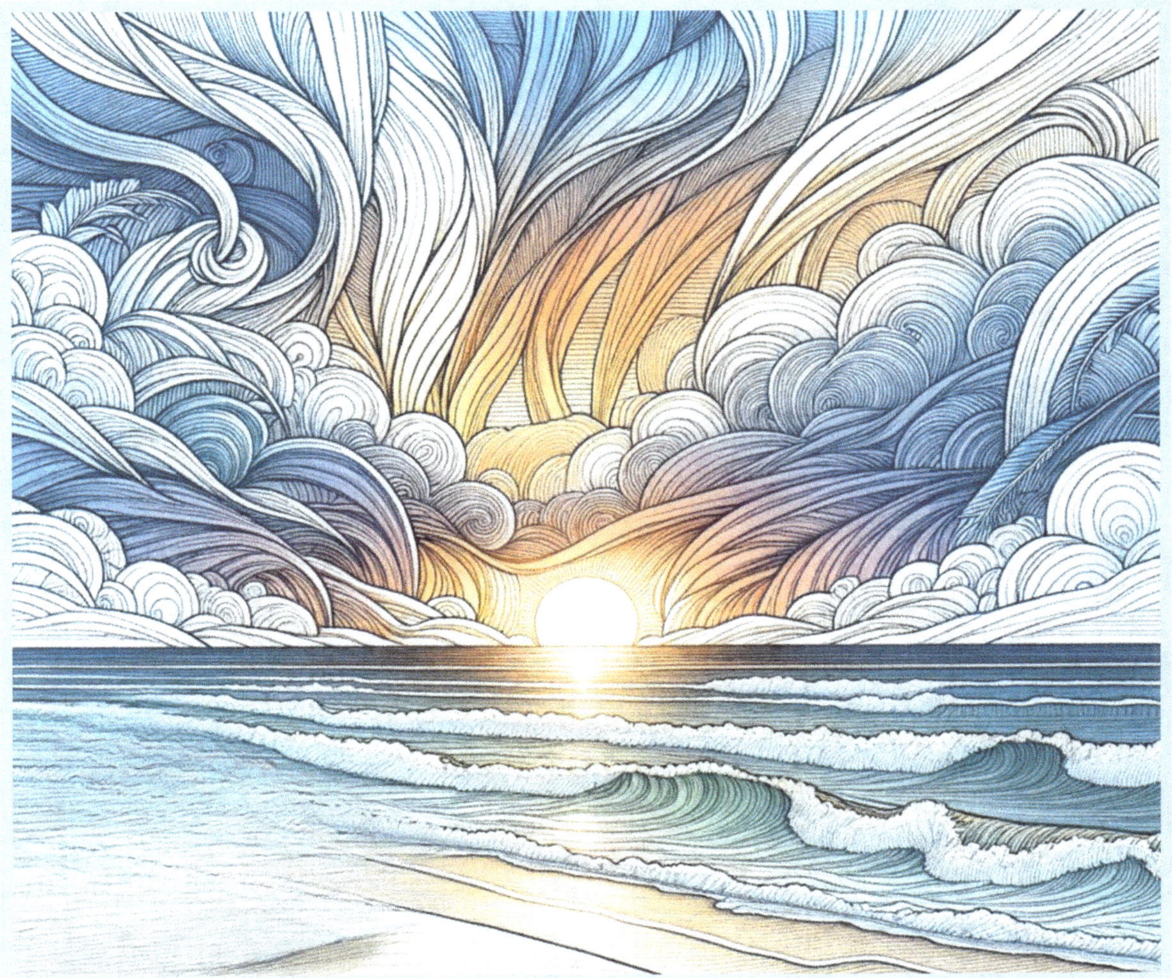

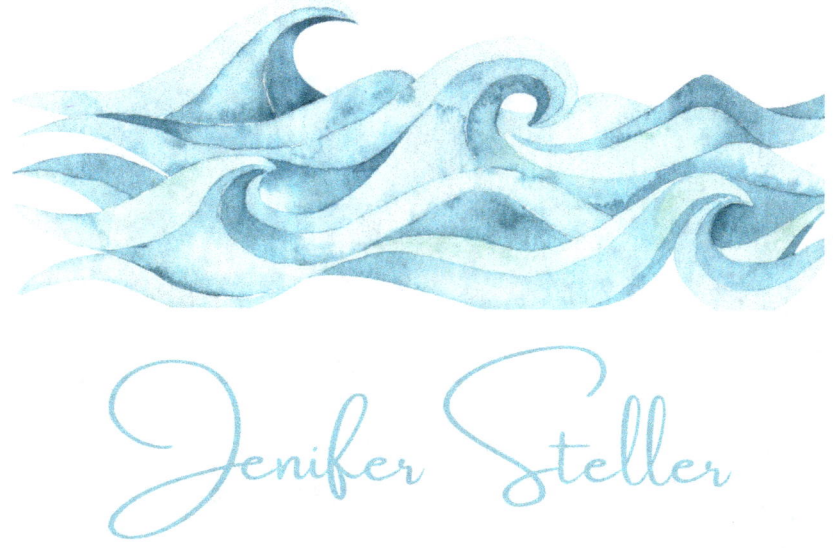

Jenifer Steller

Creative concepts developed in the organization and writing of this book are the creative and intellectual property of Jenifer J. Steller. All materials are commercially licensed.

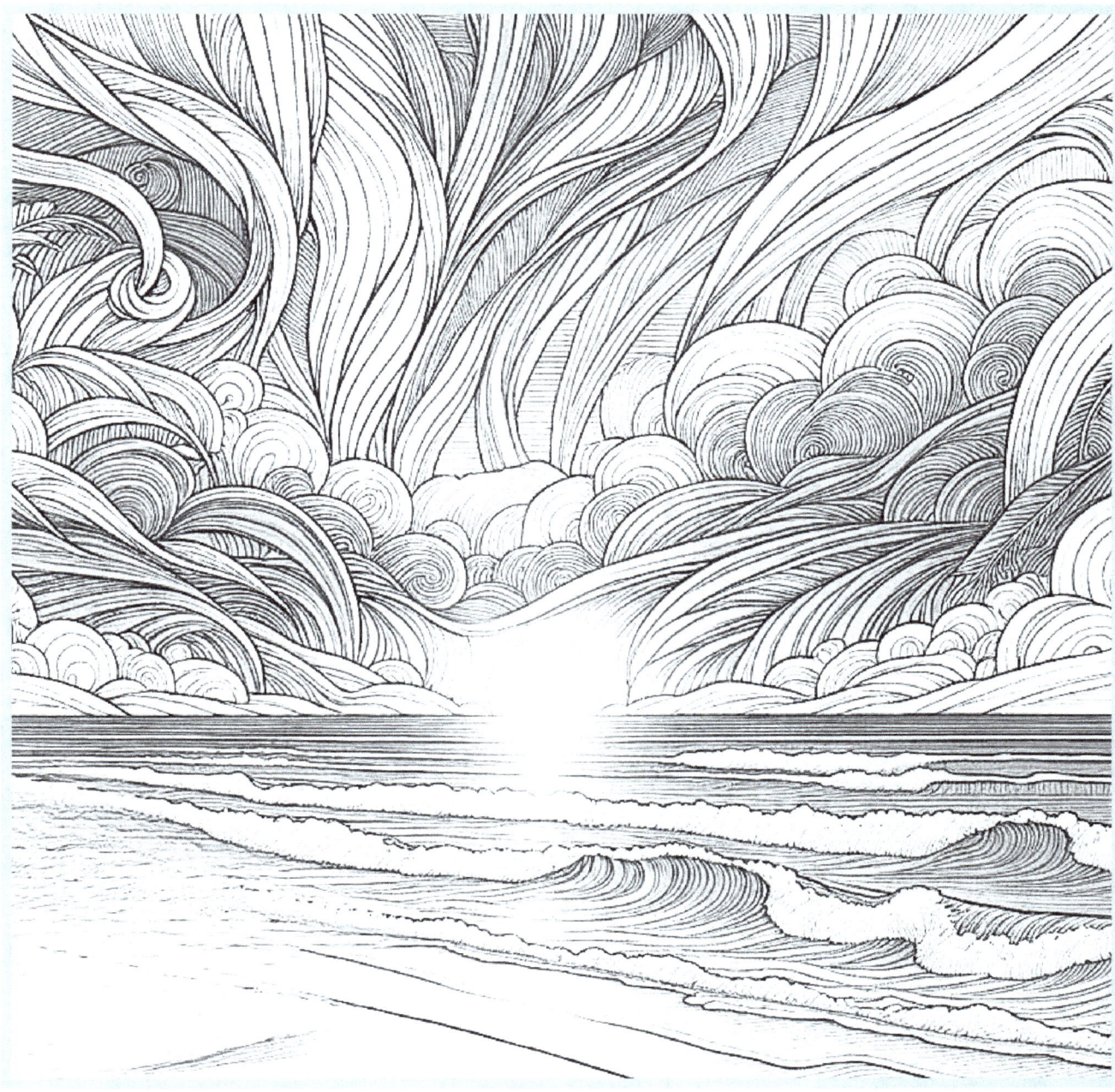

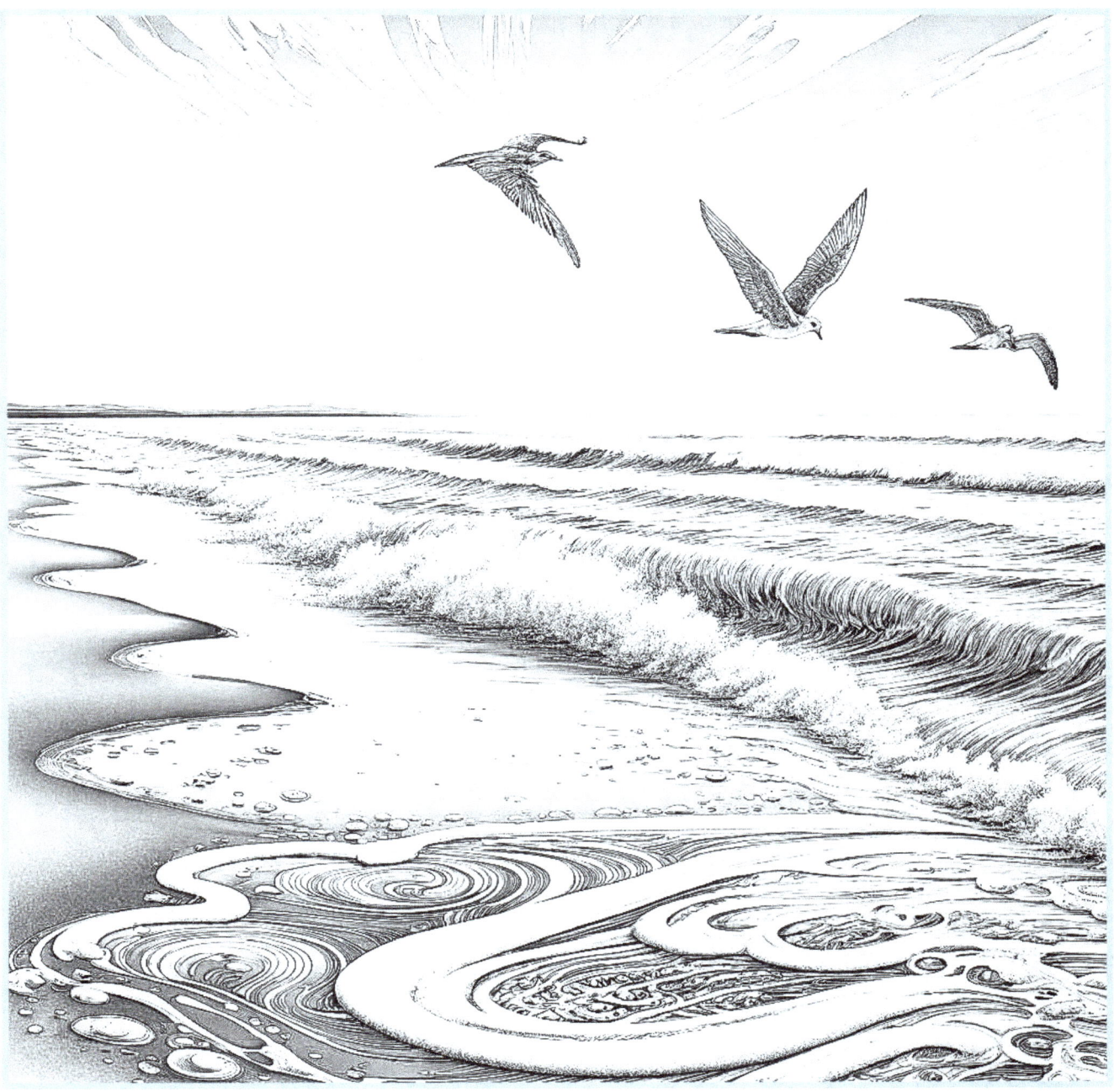

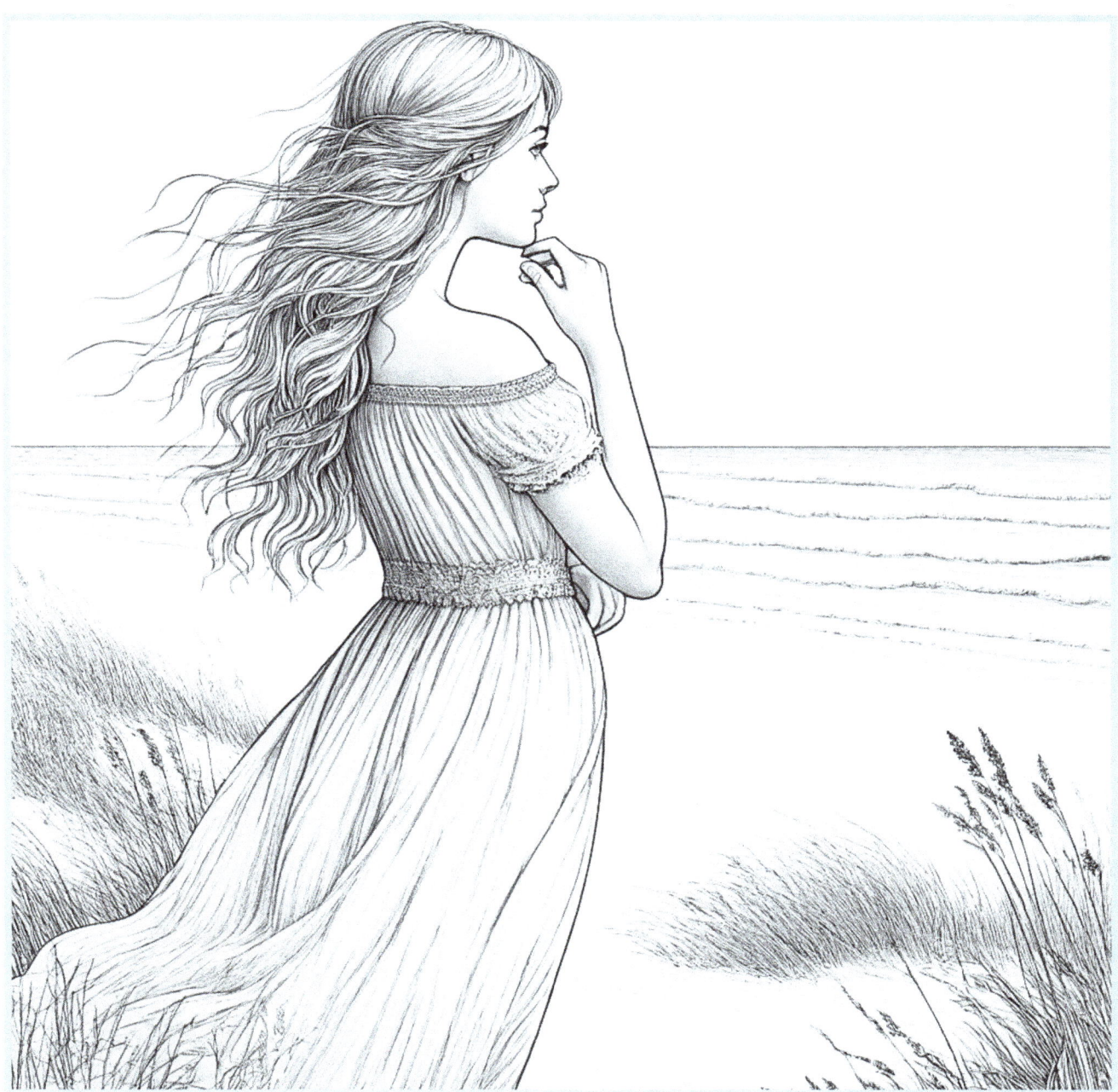

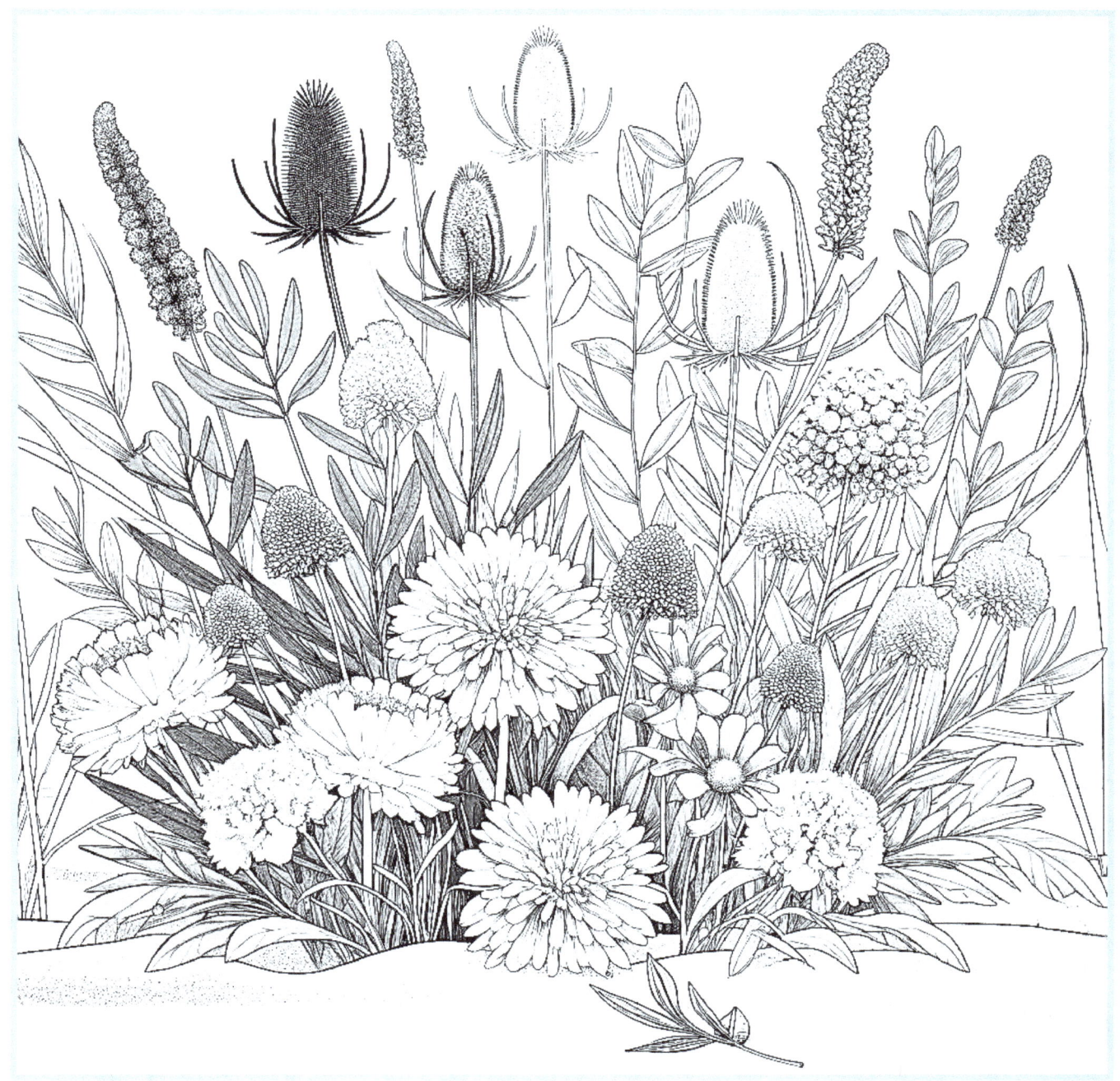

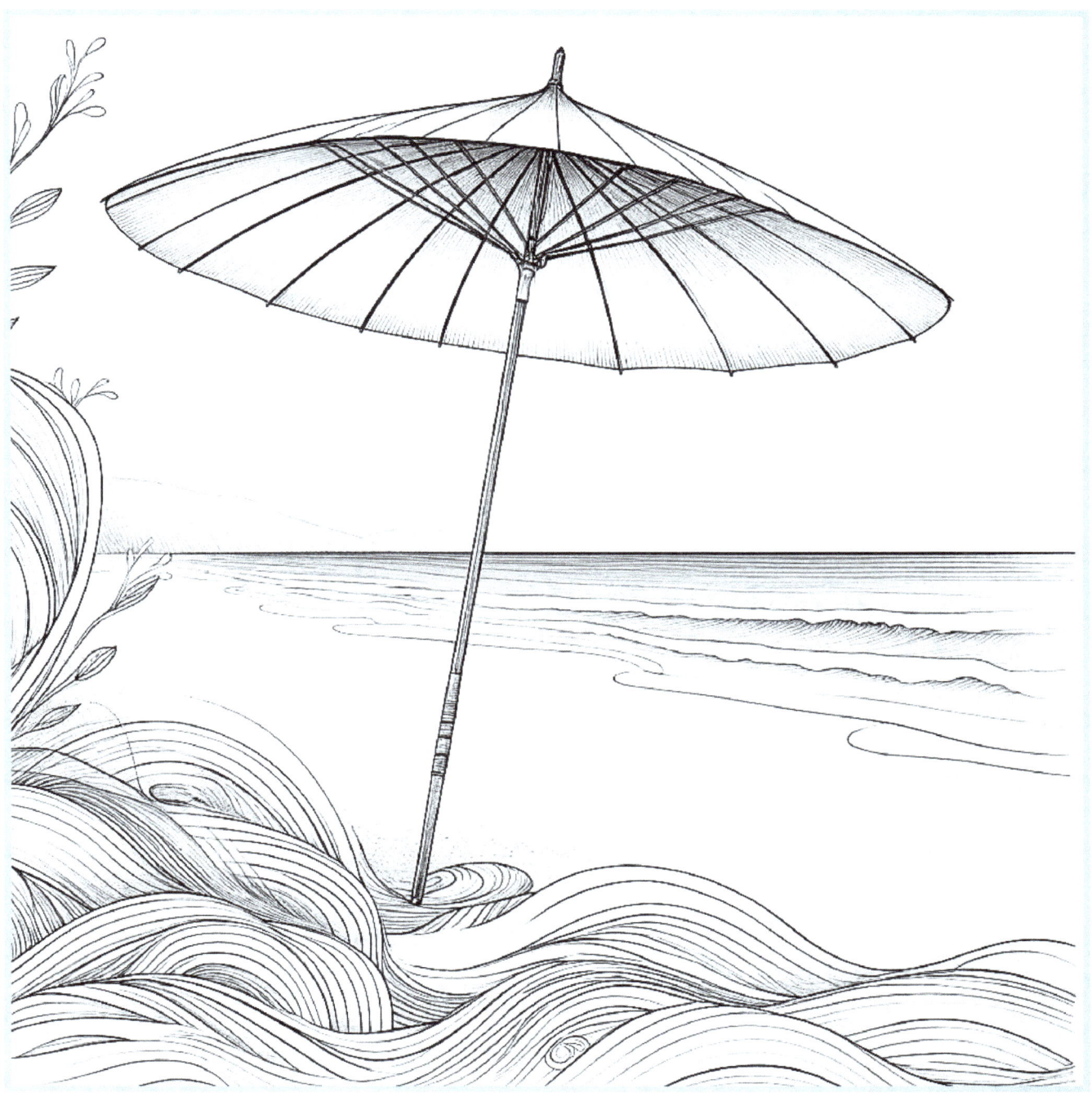

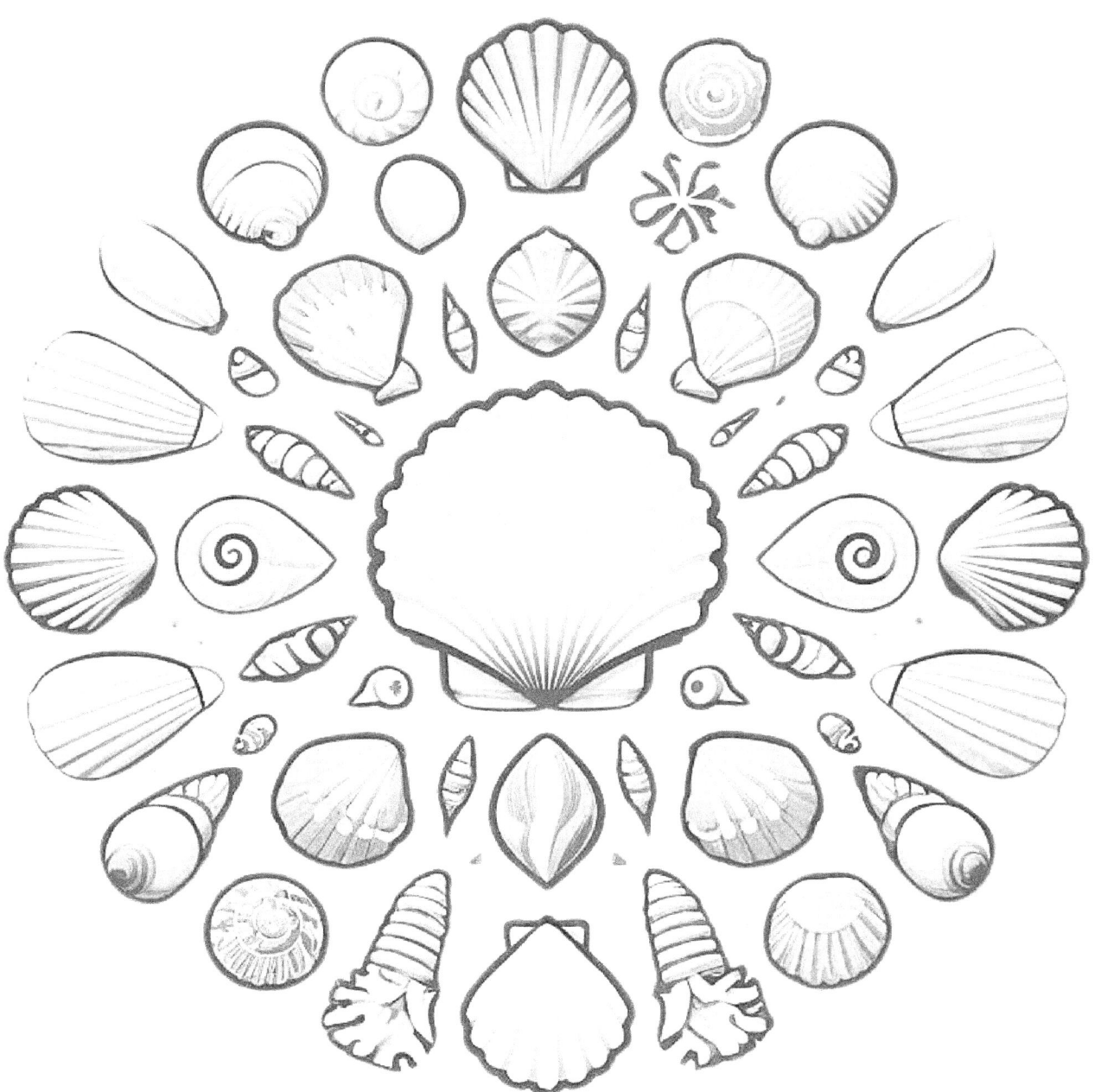

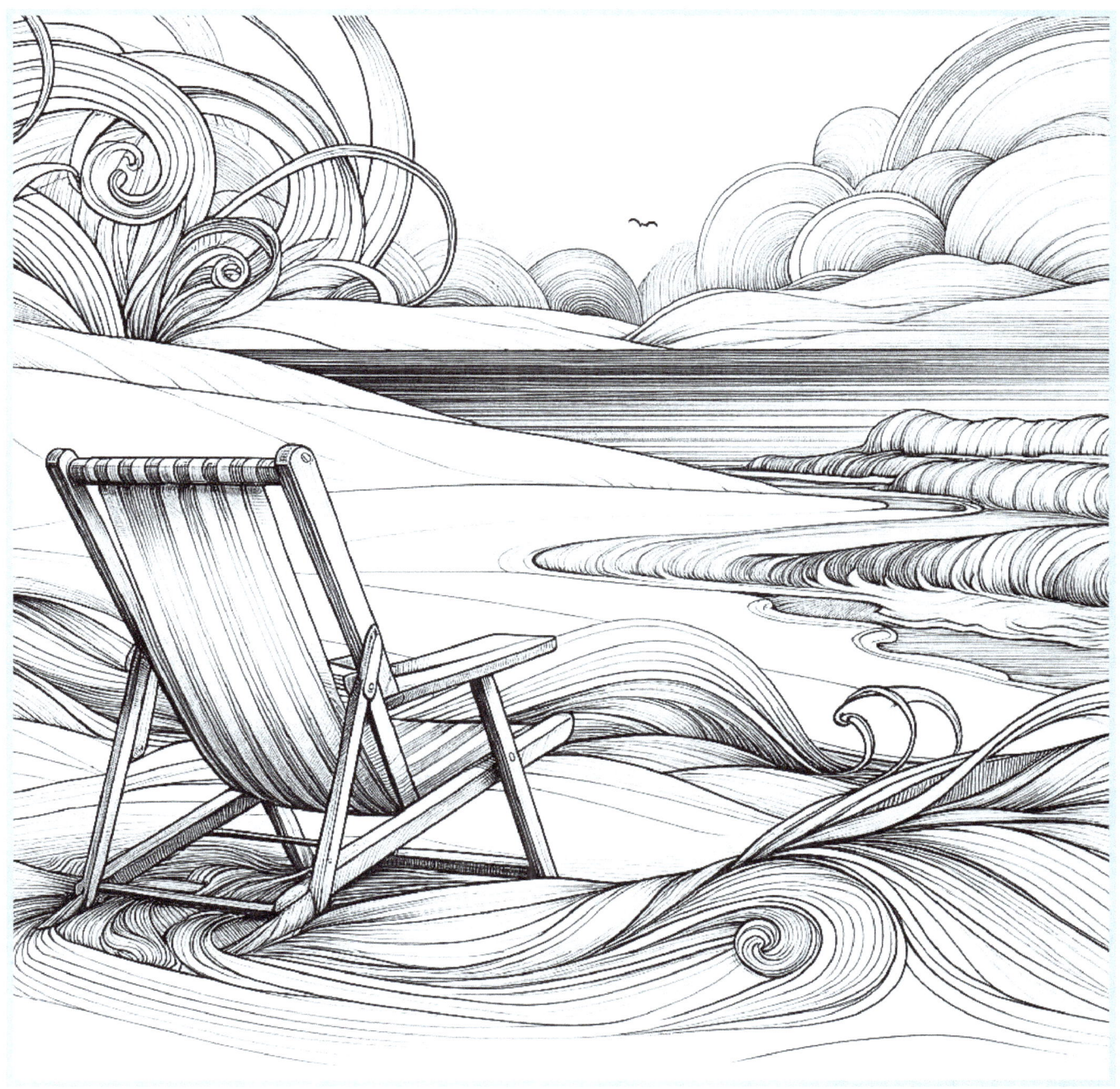

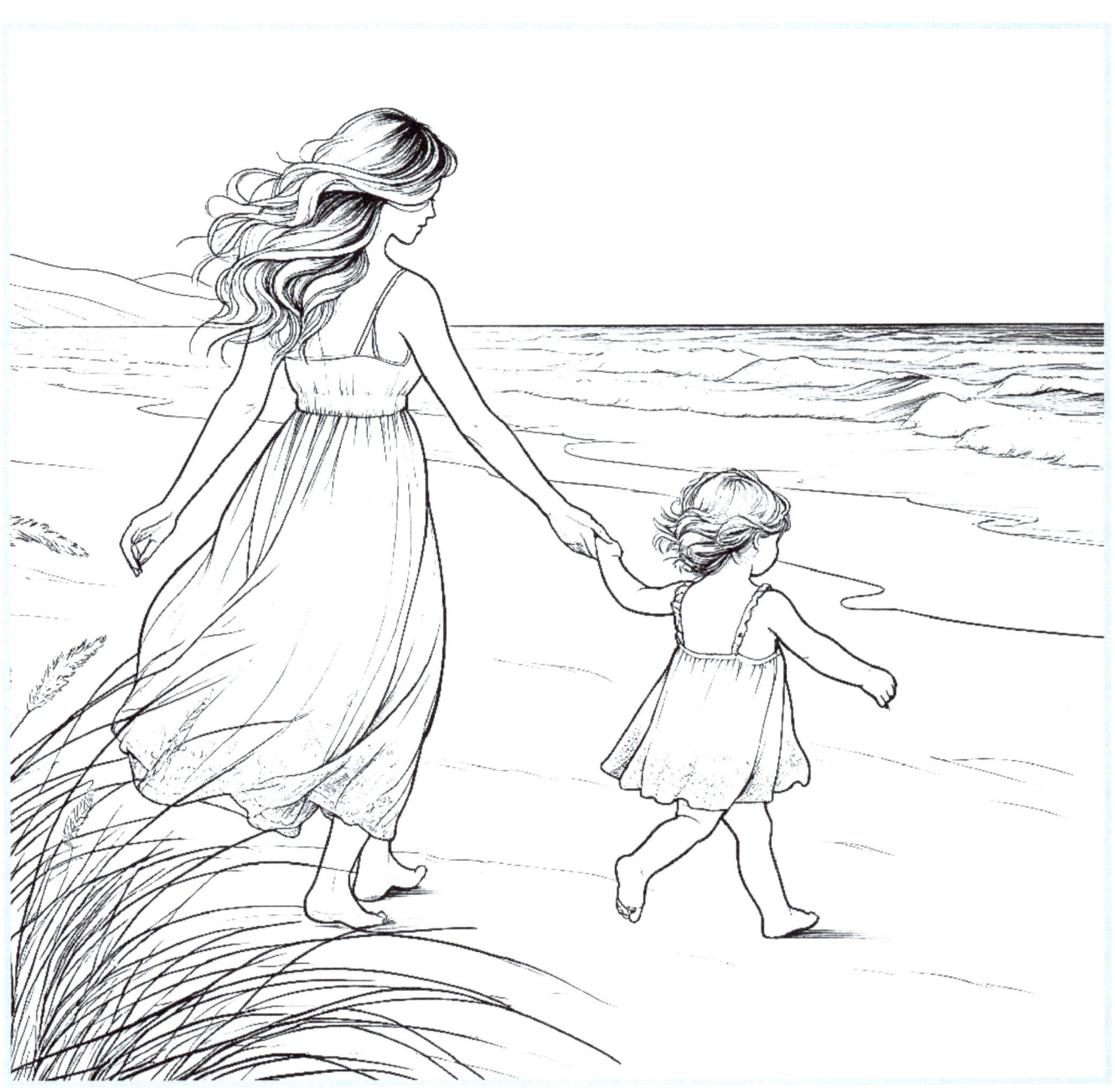

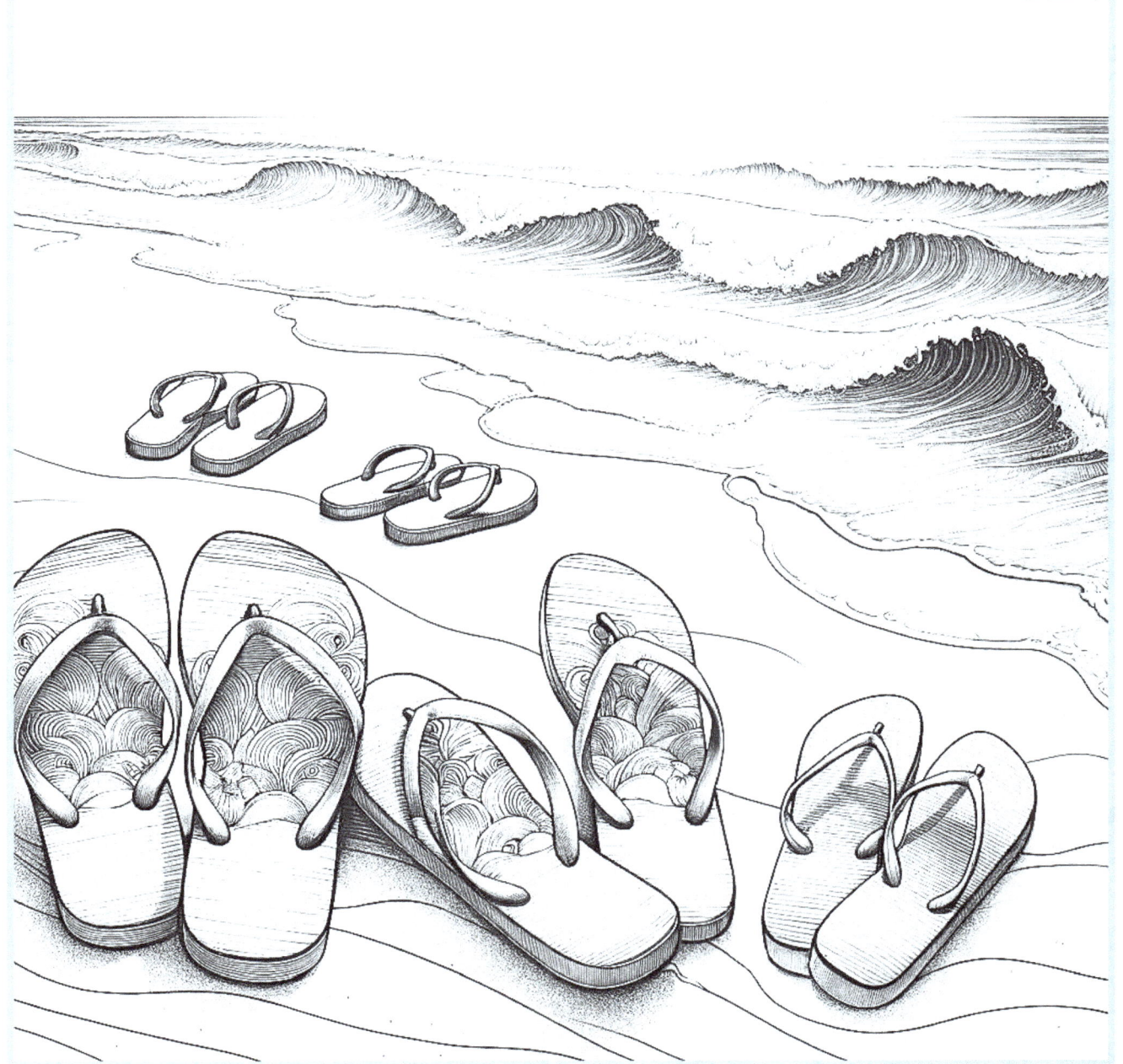

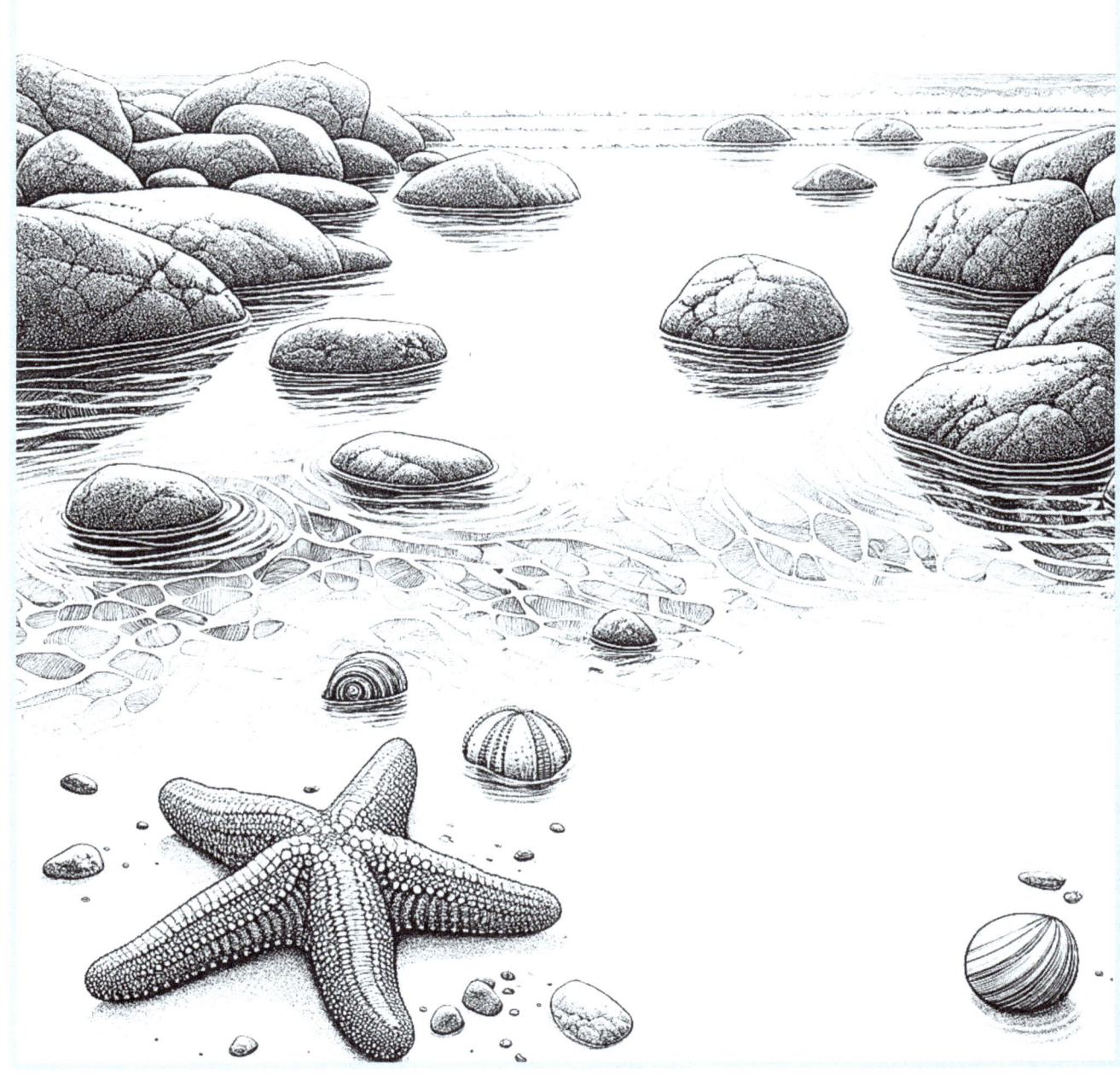

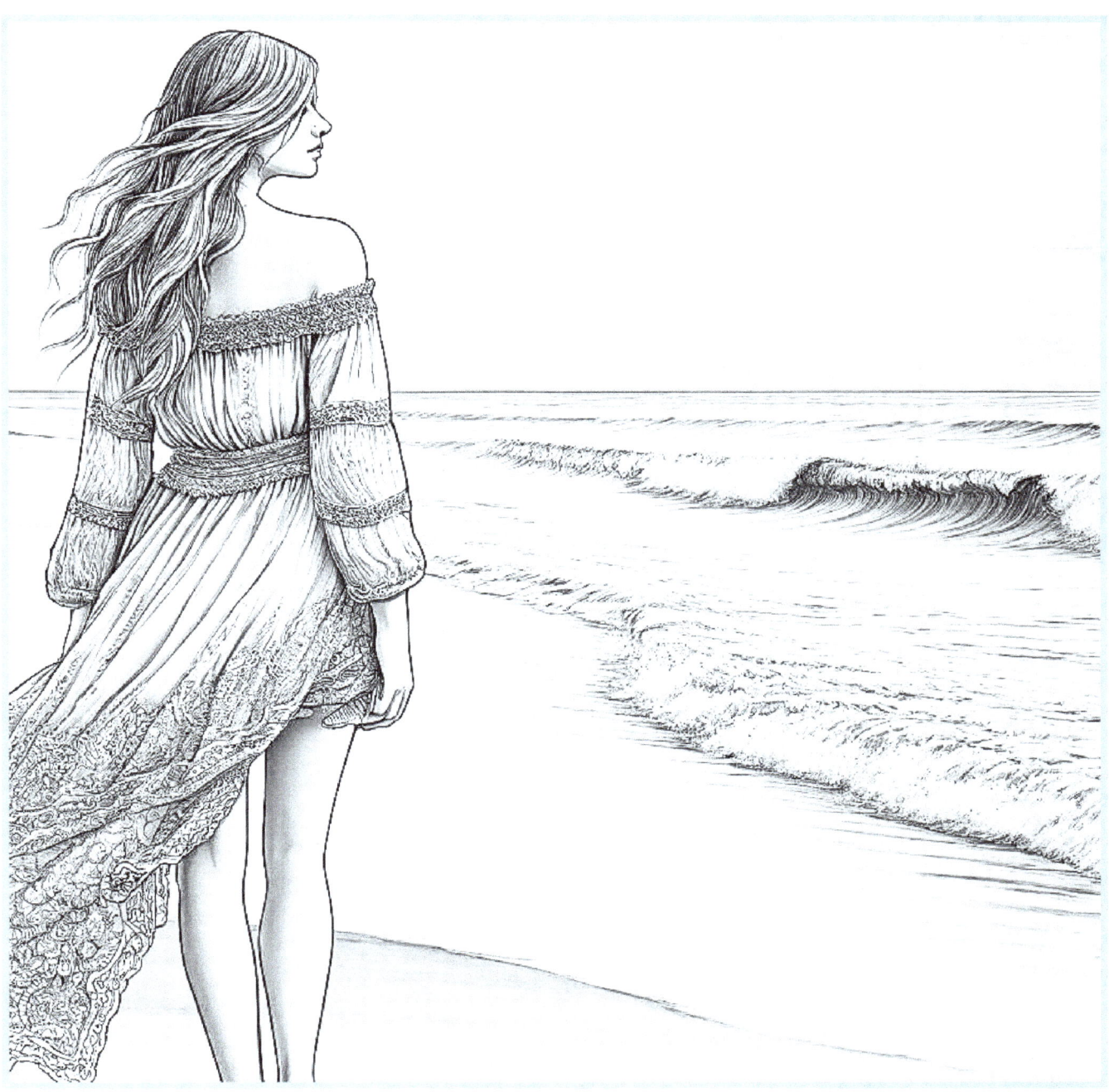

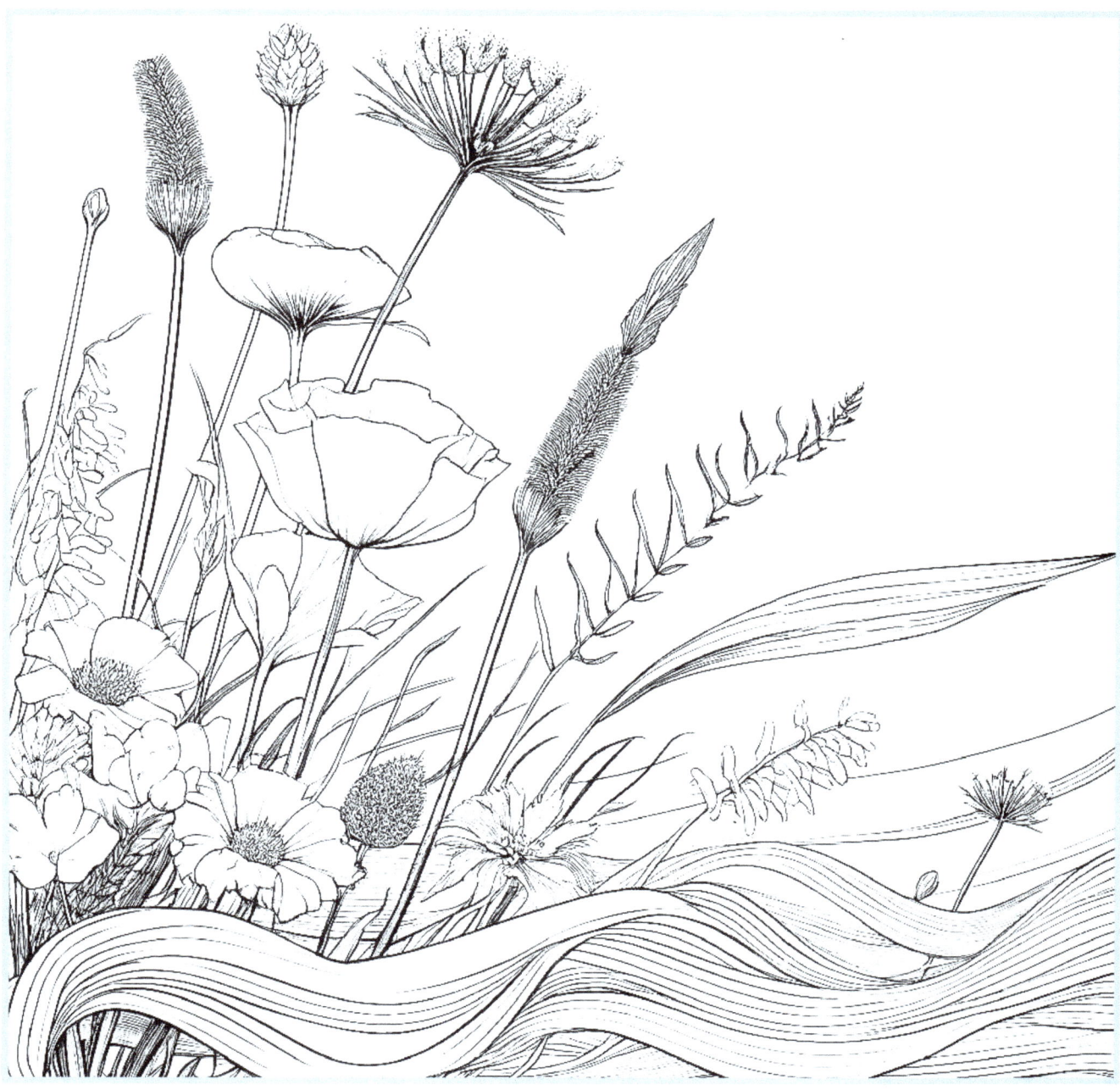

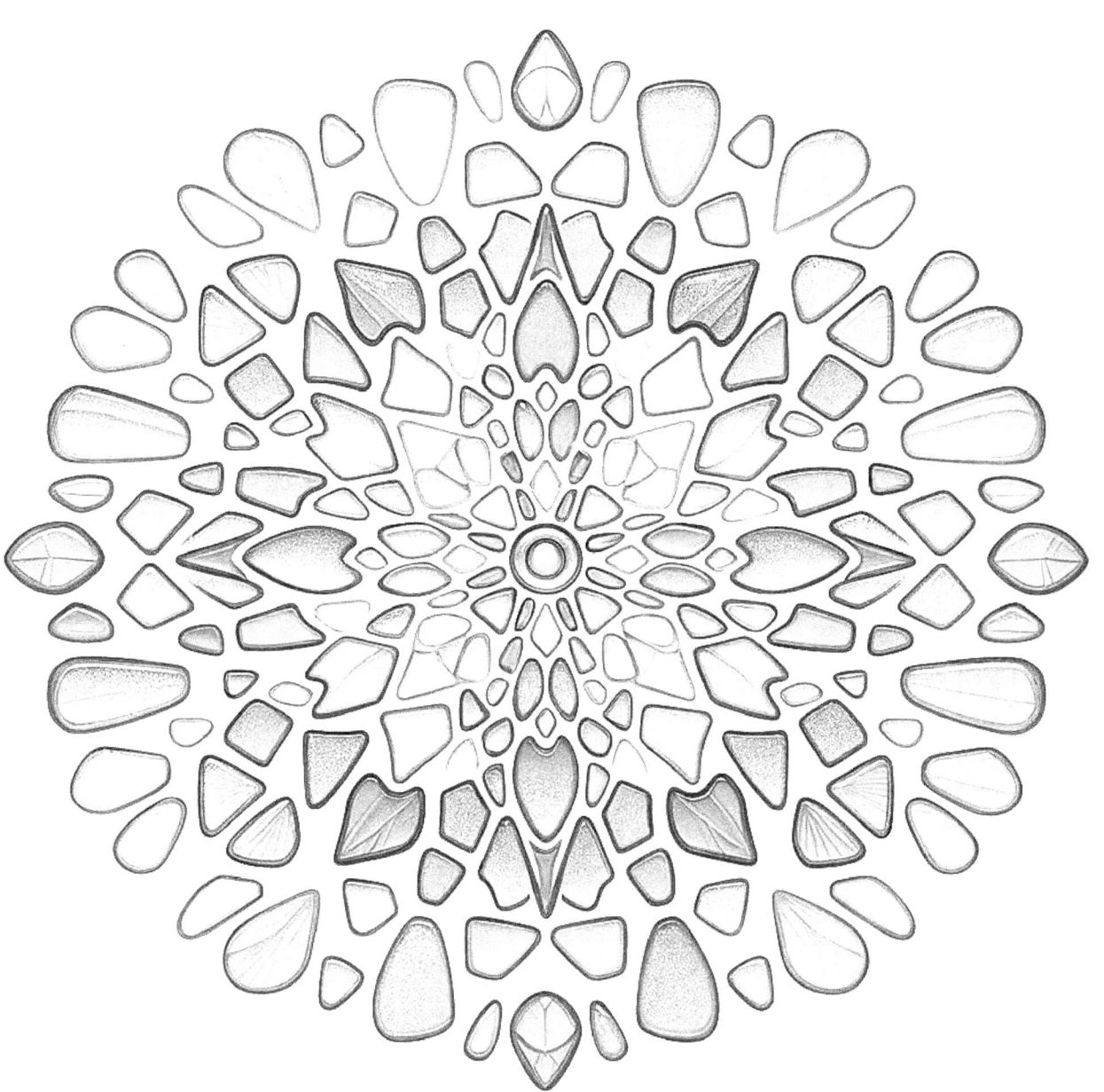

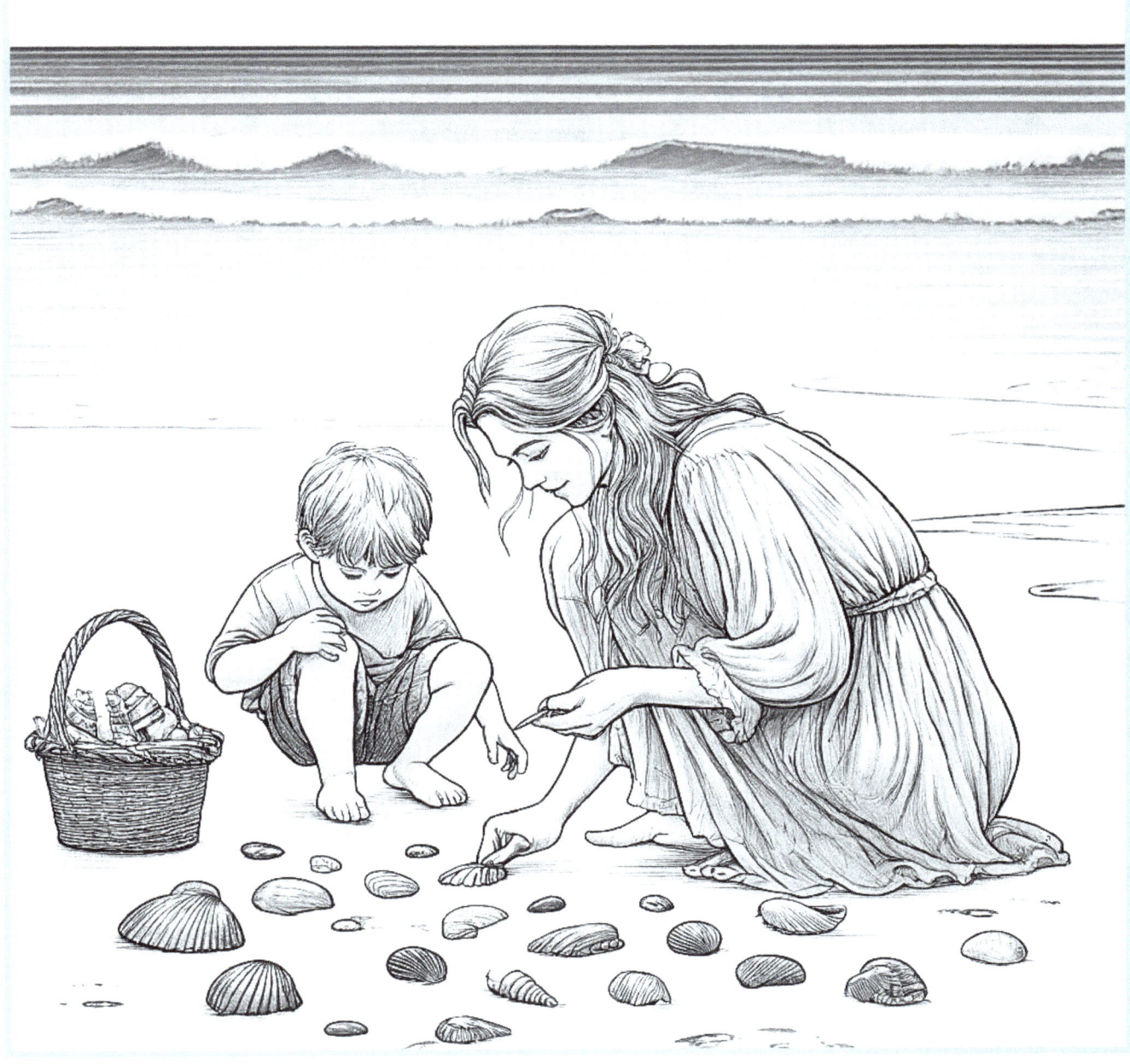

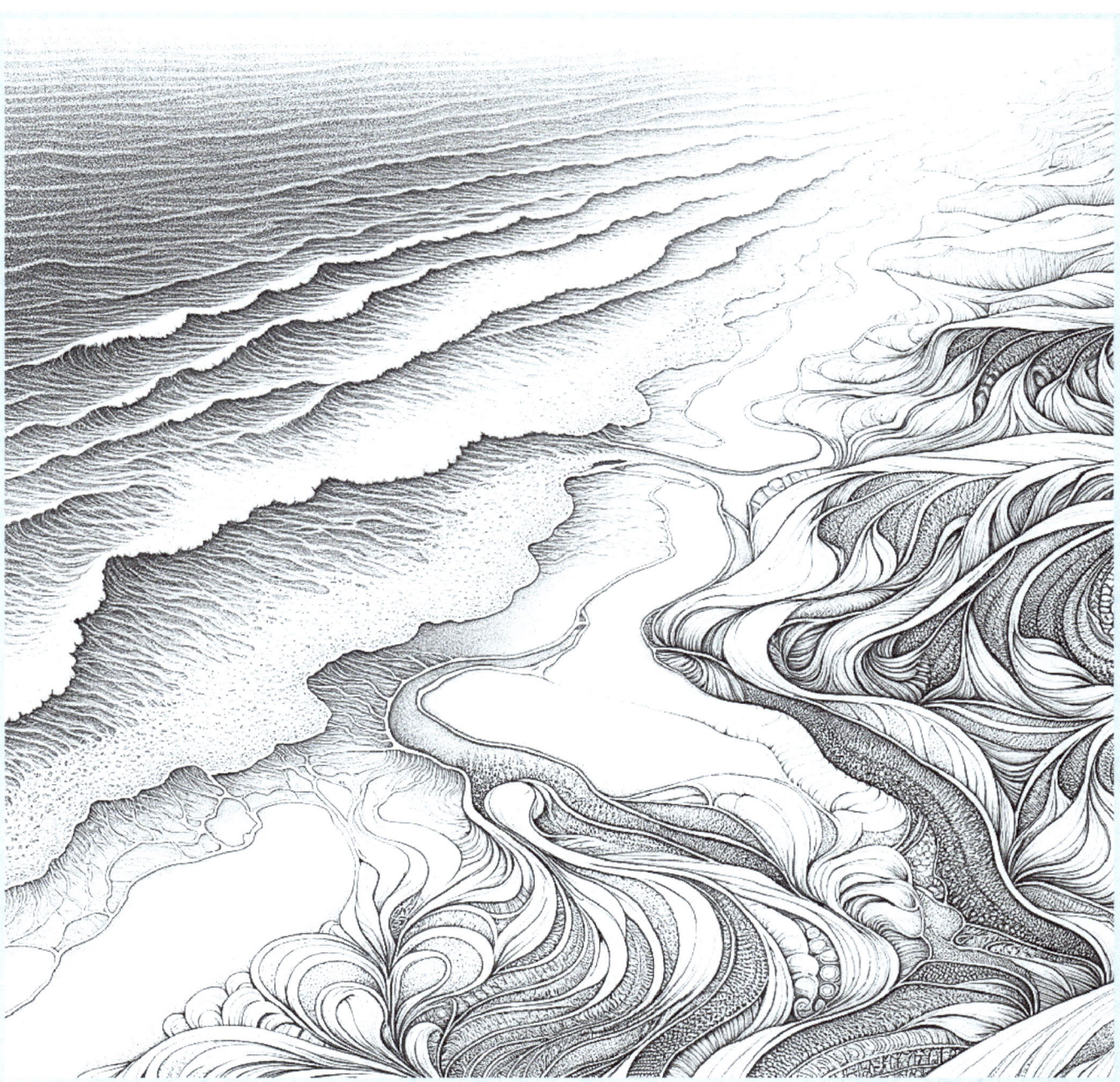

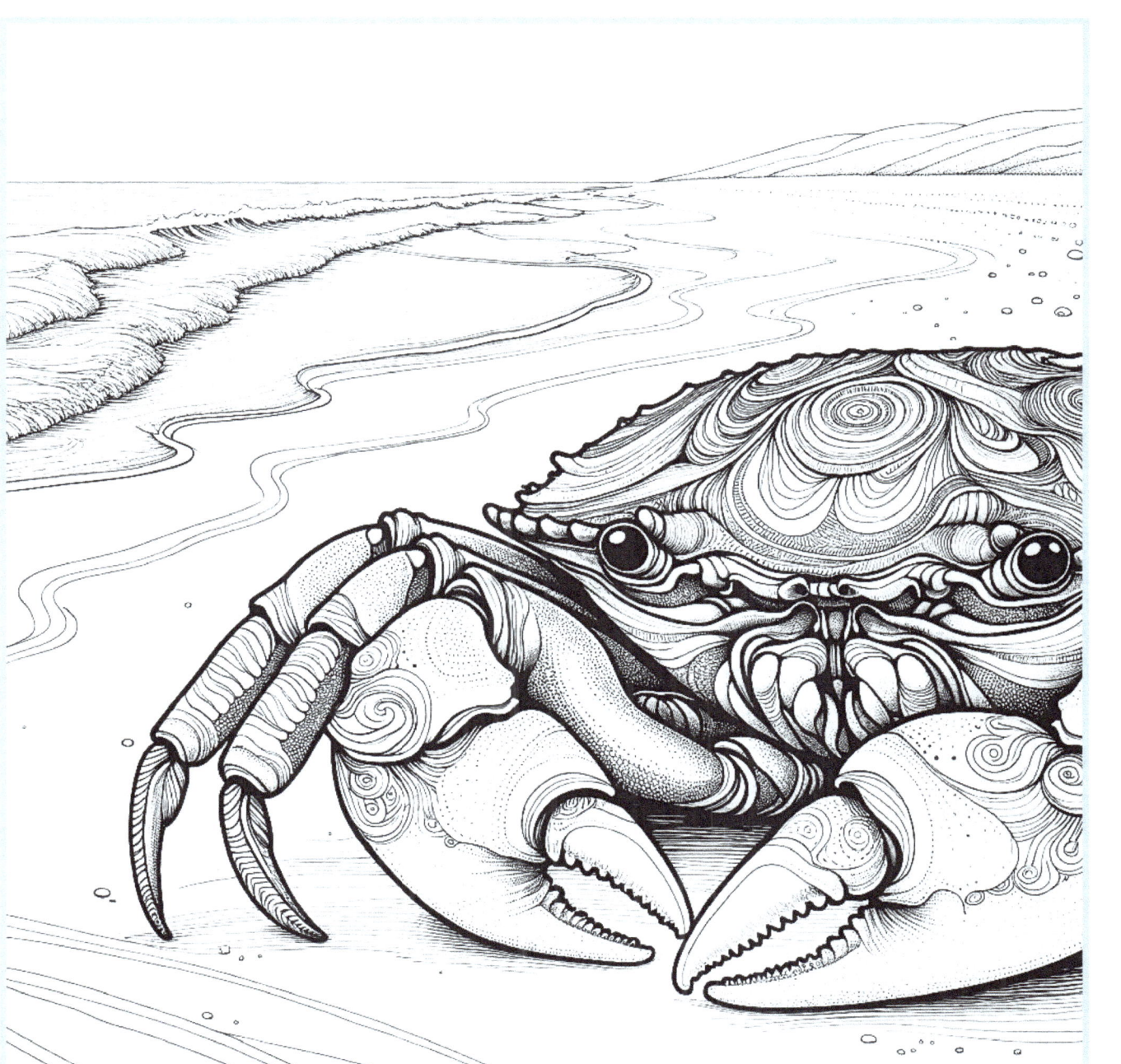

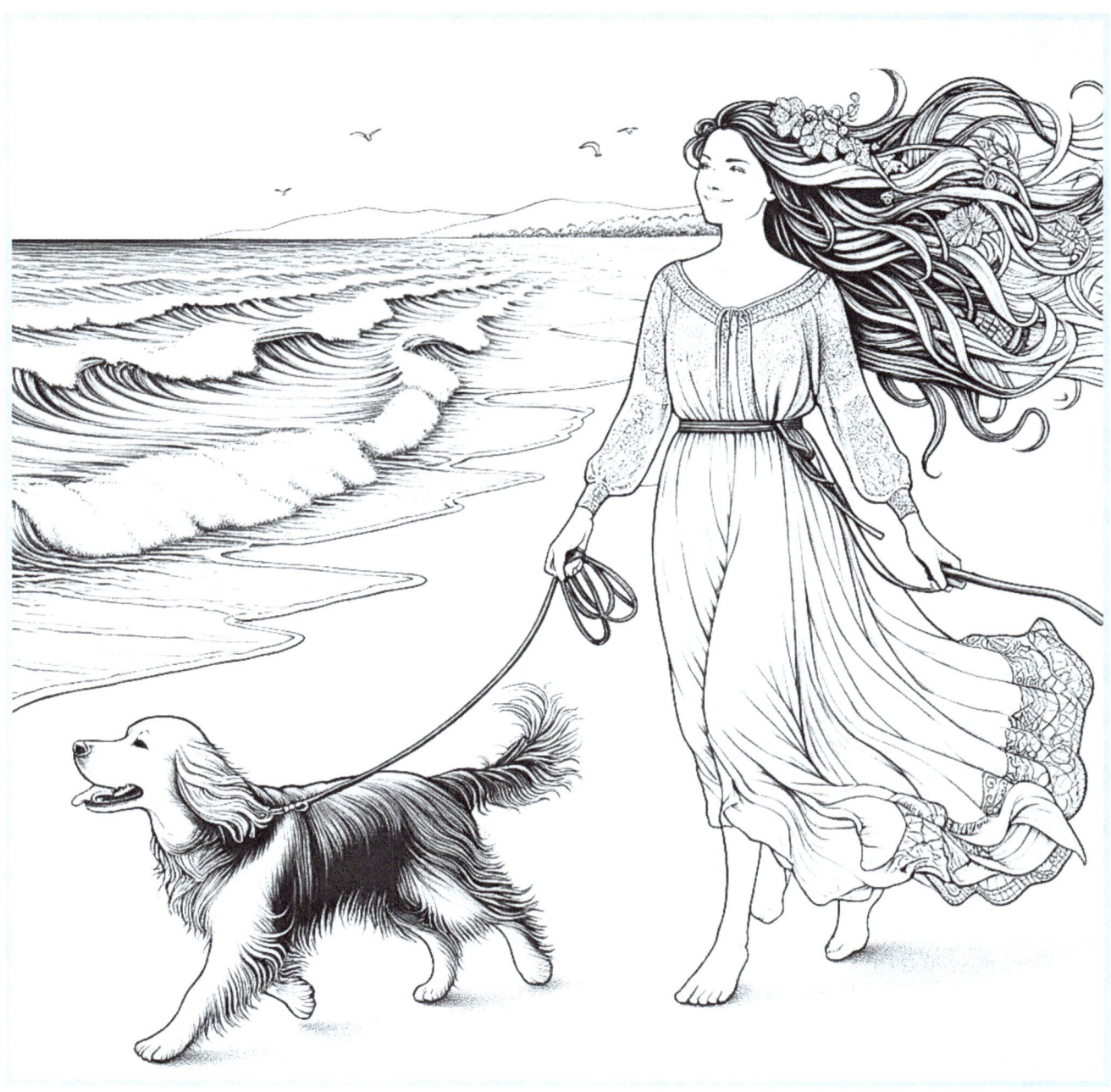

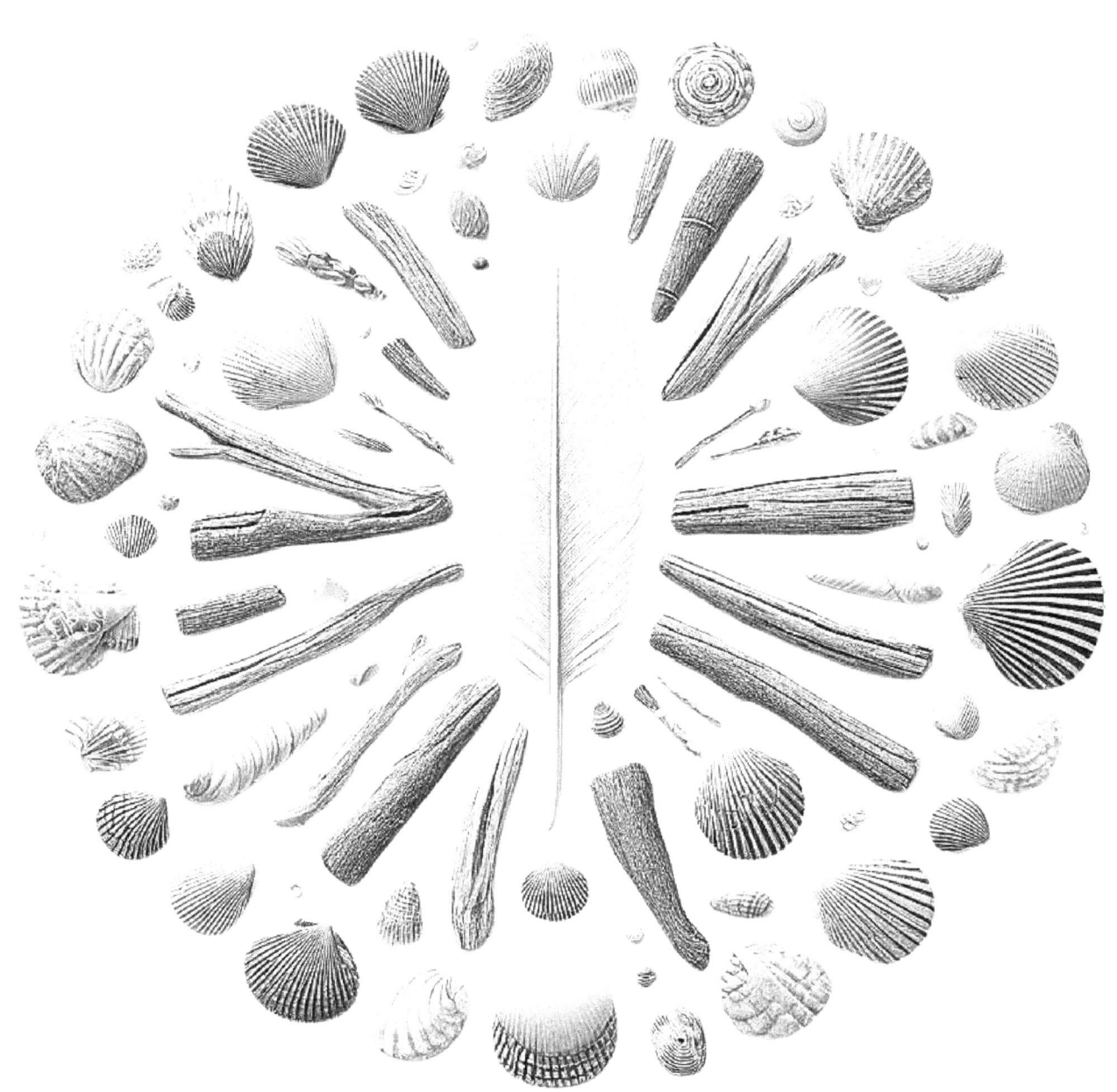

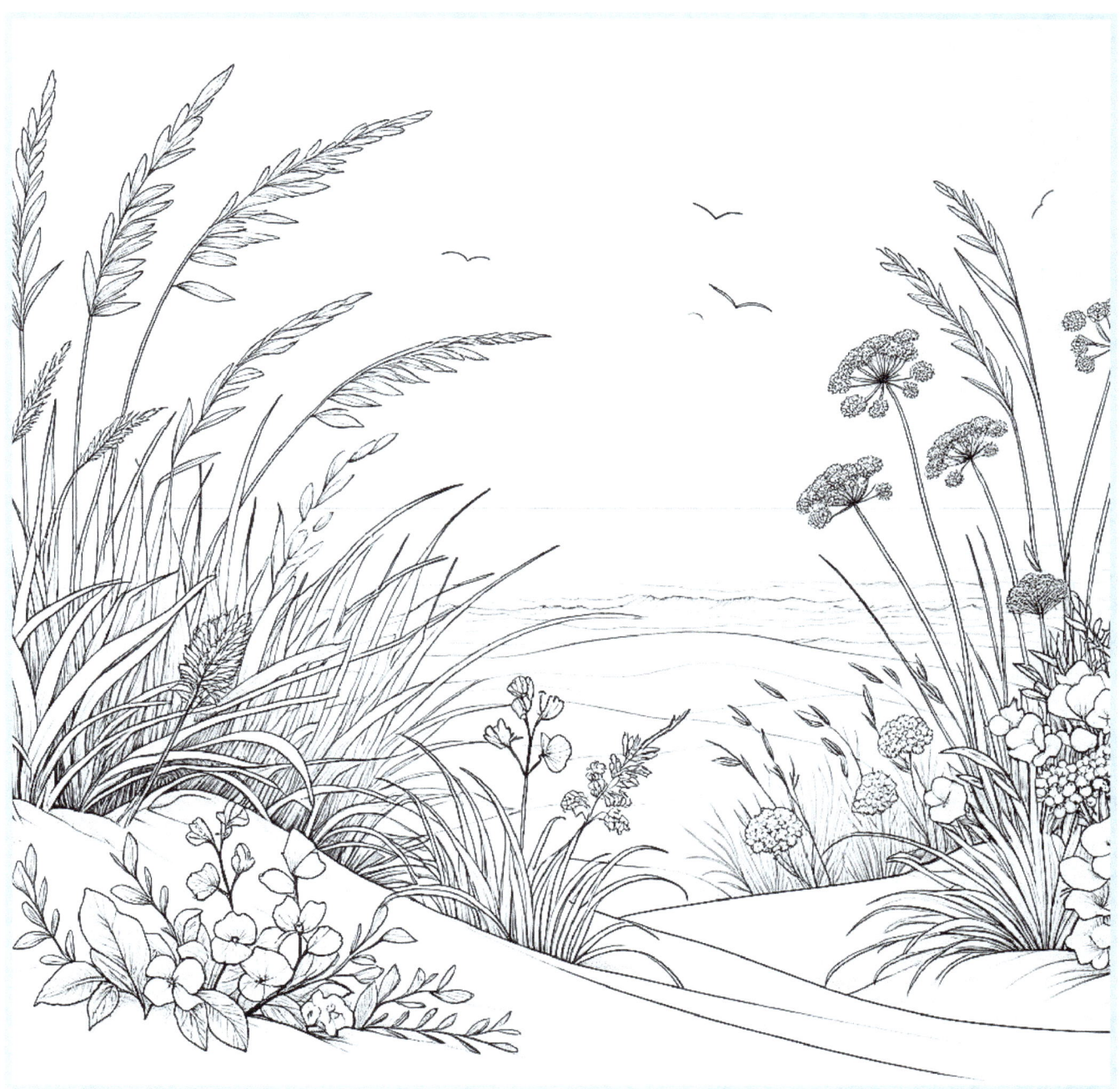

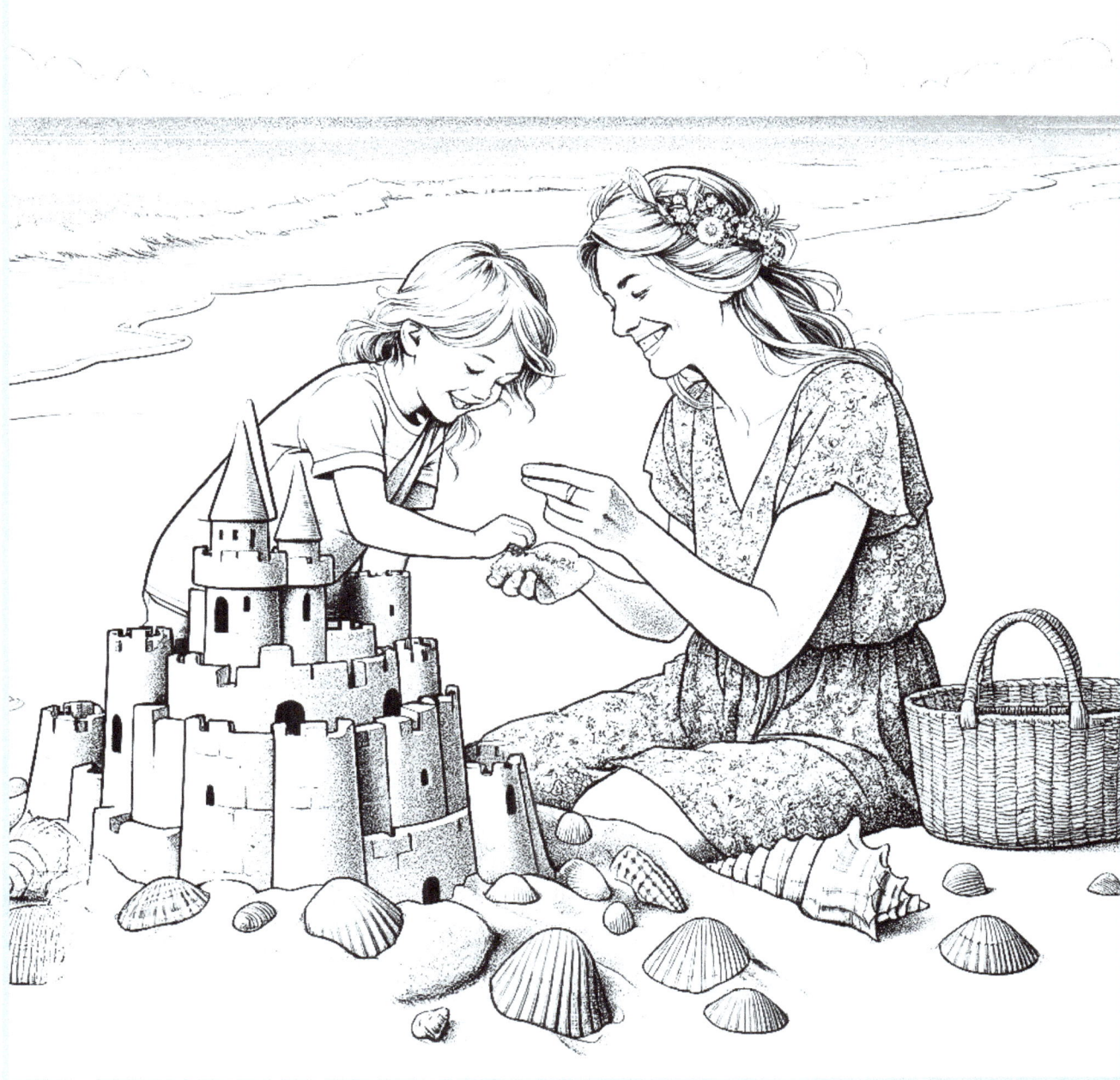

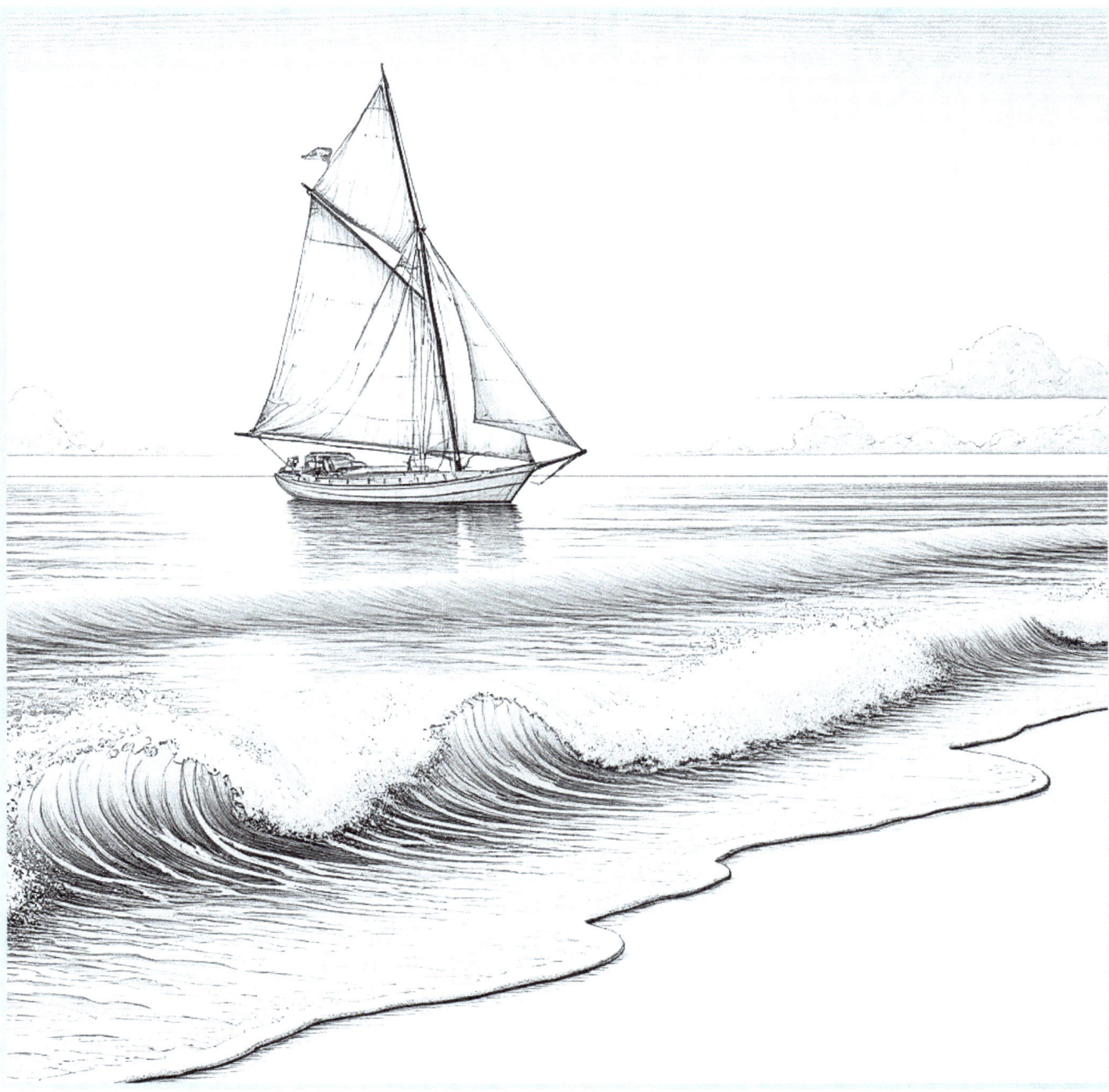

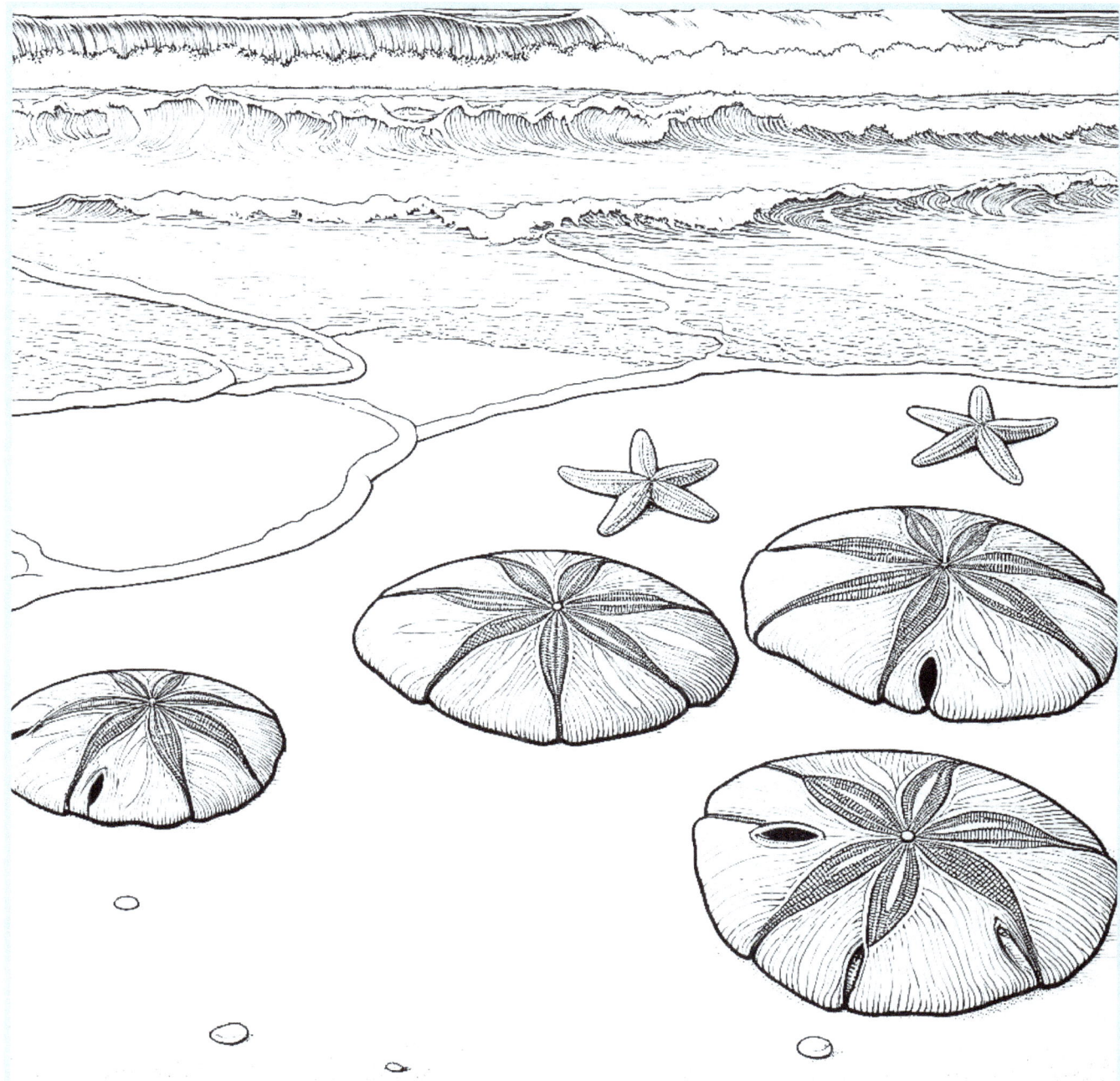

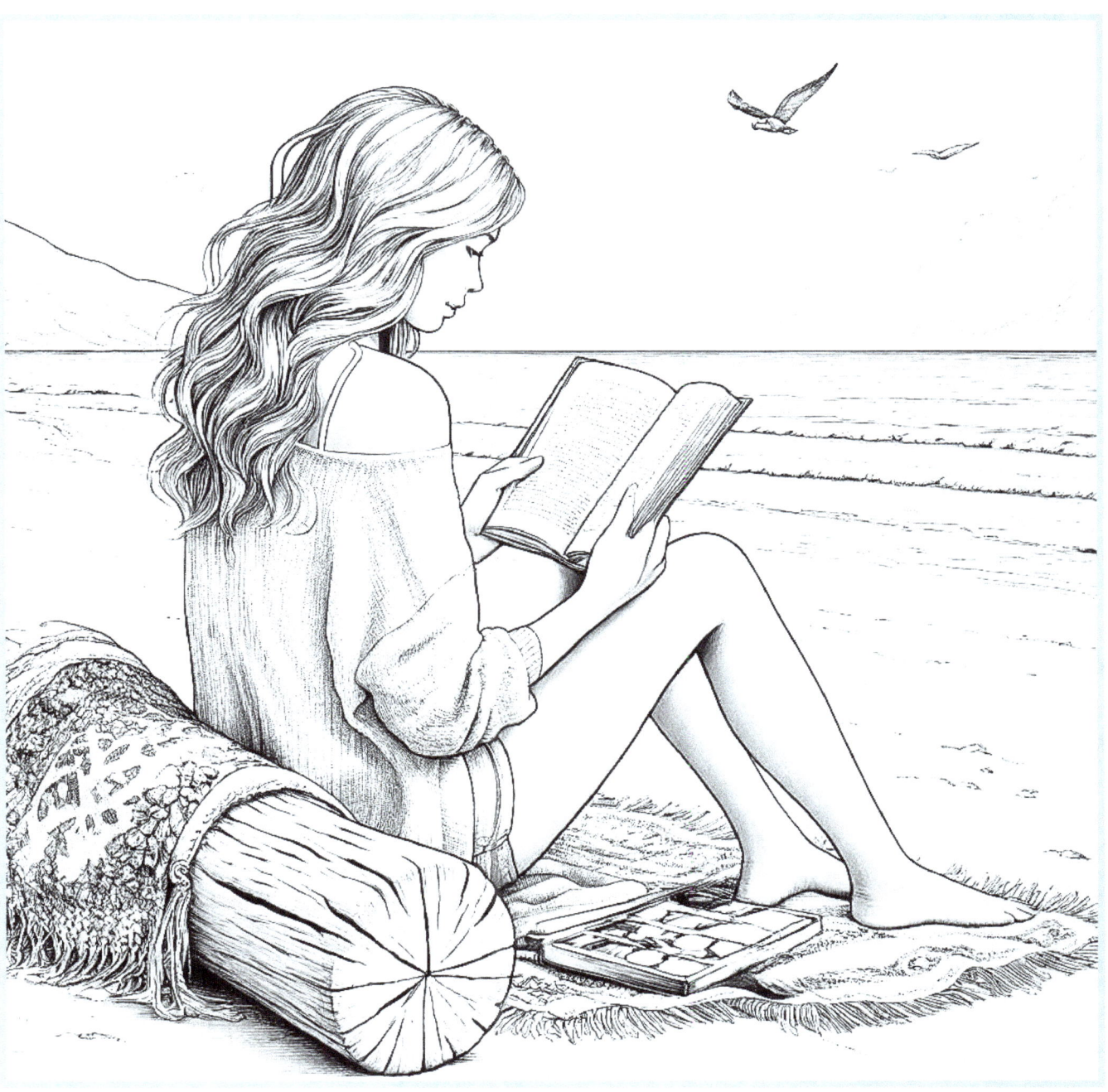

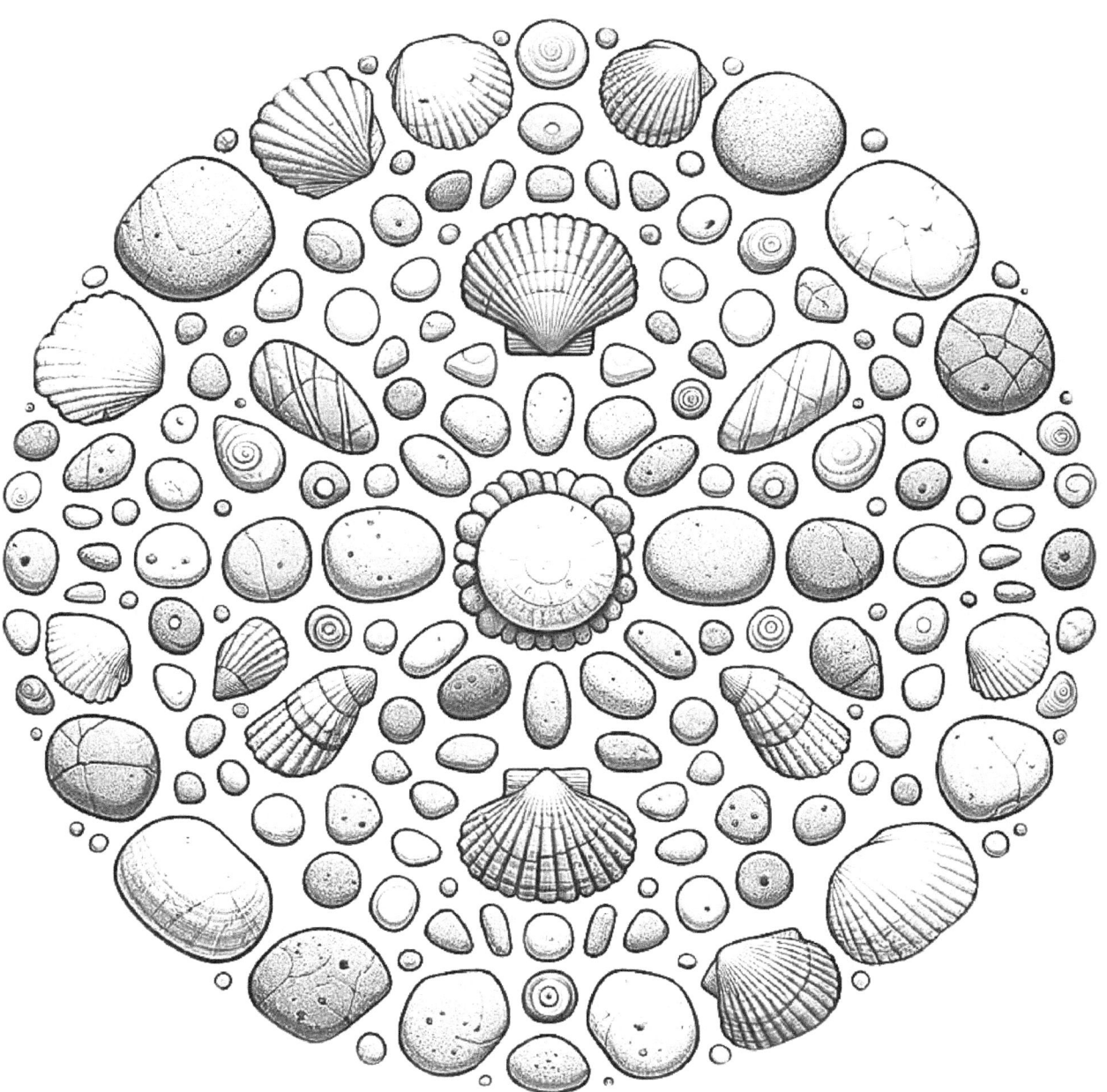

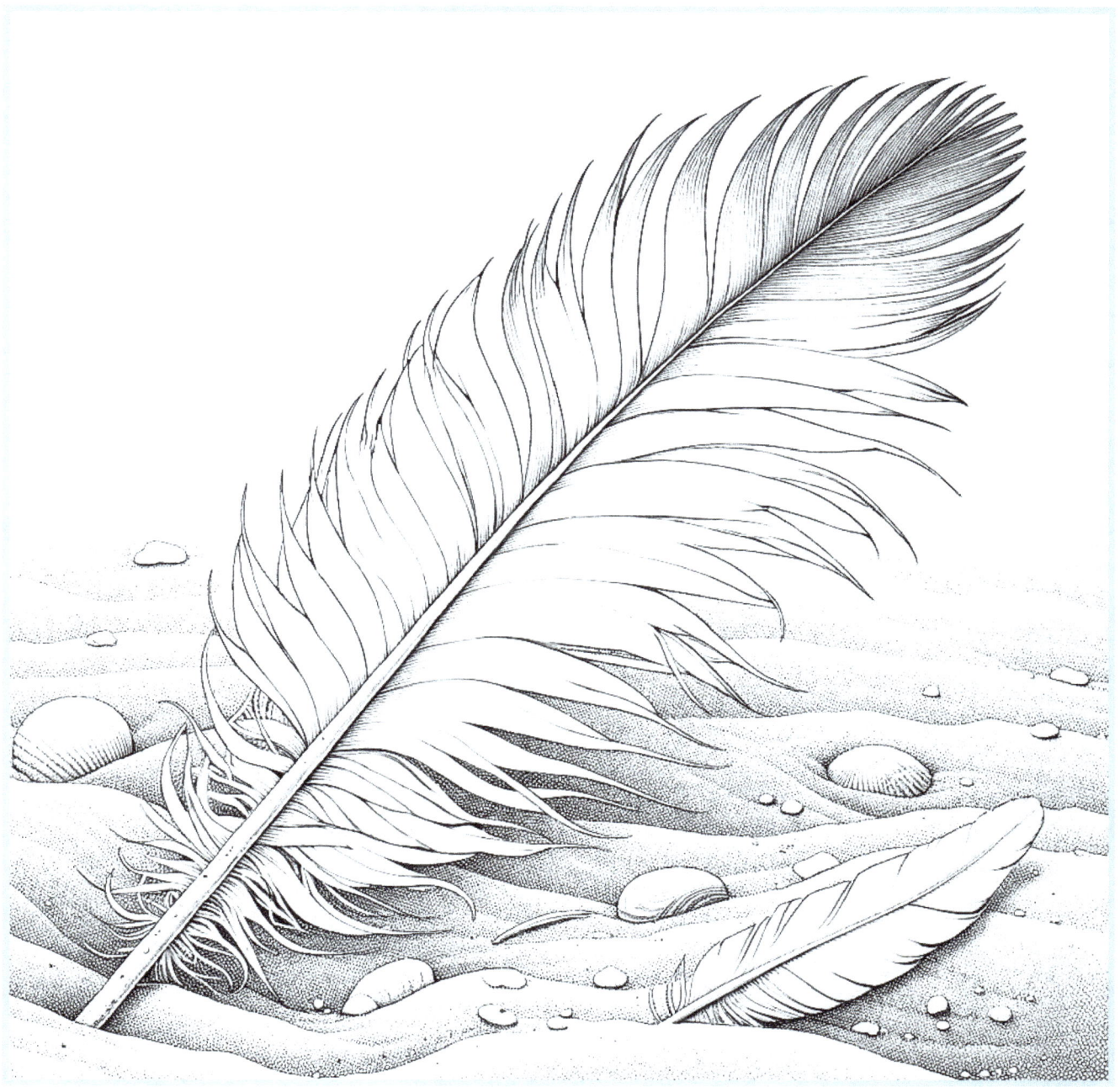

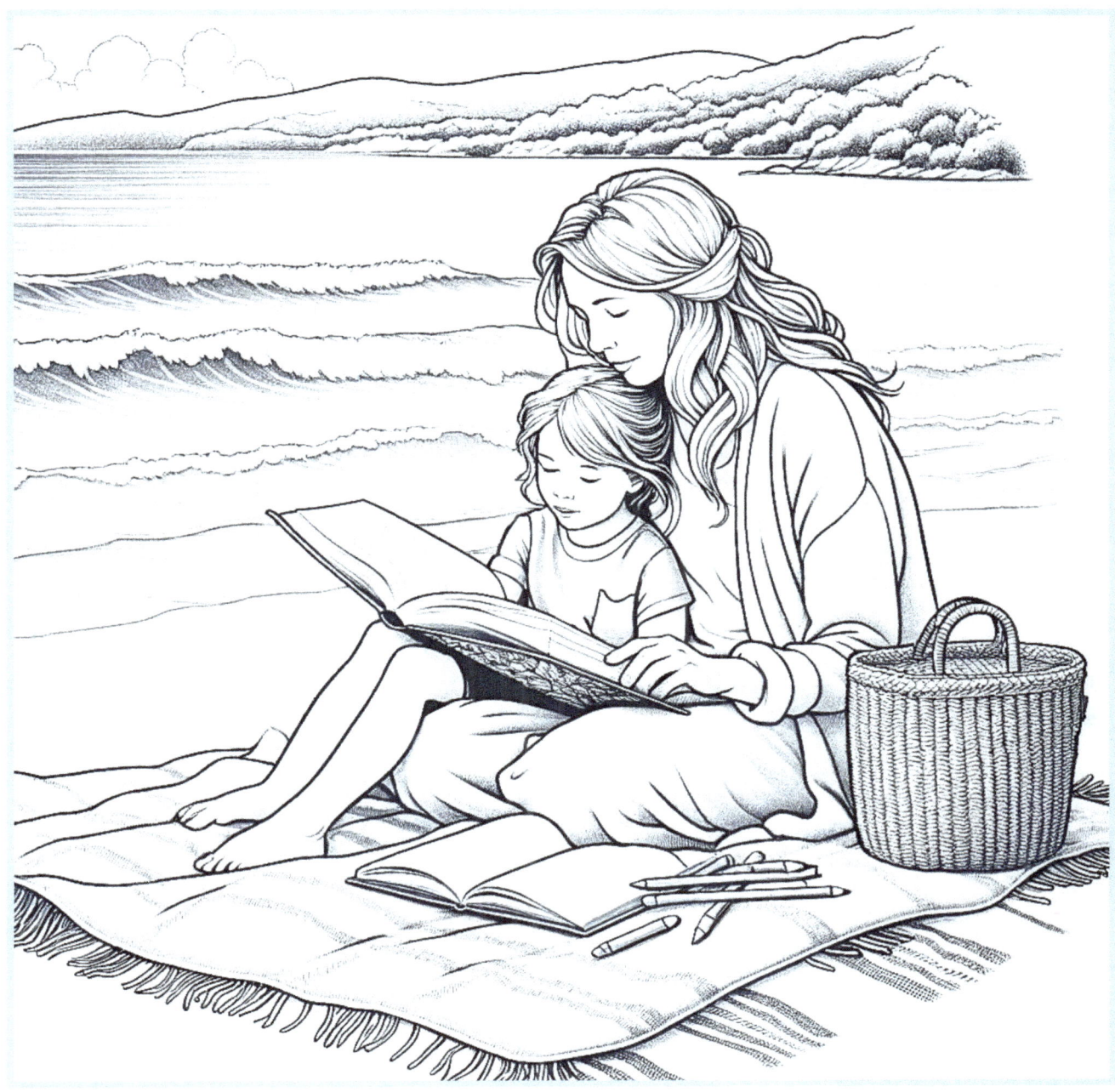

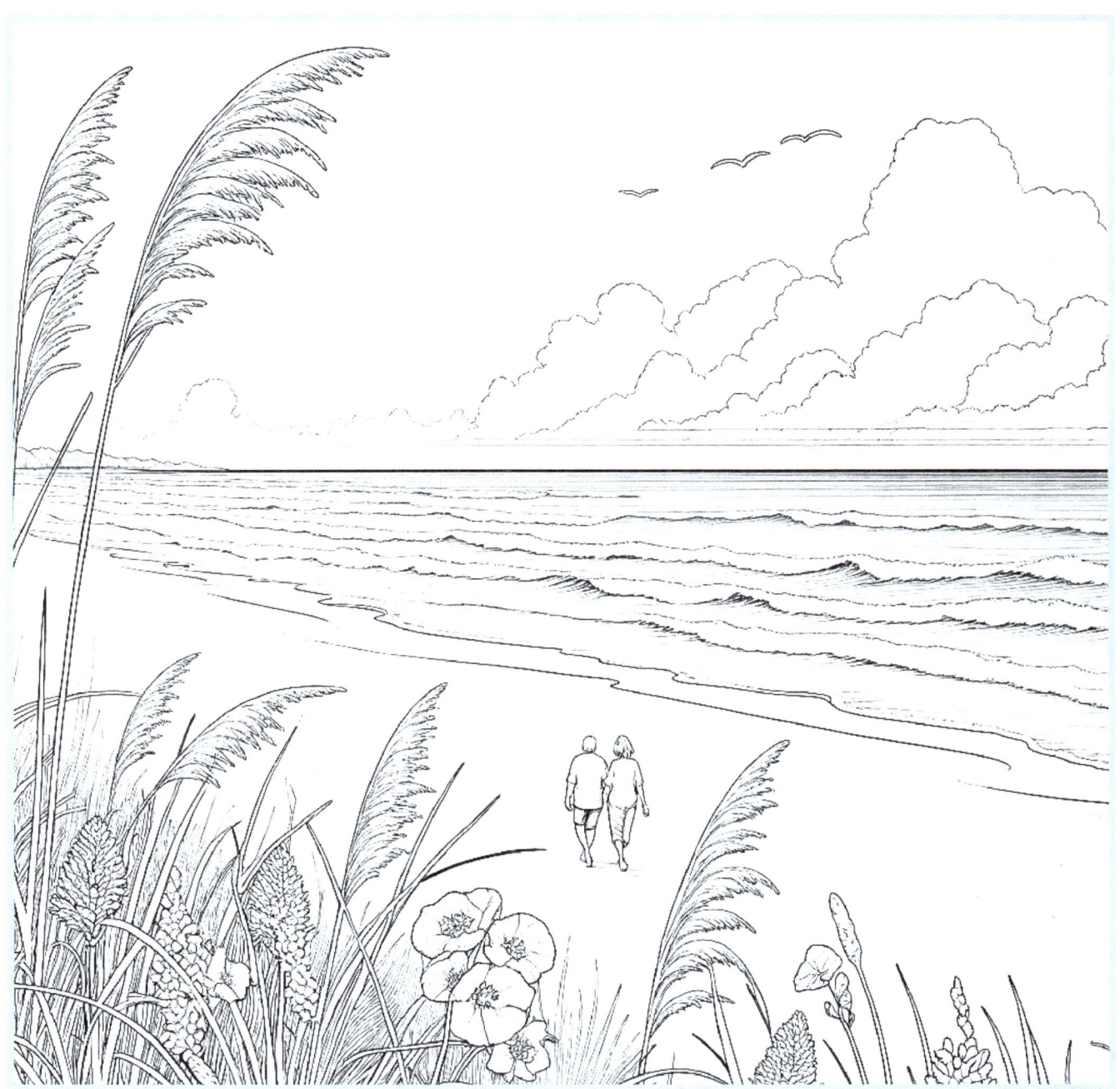

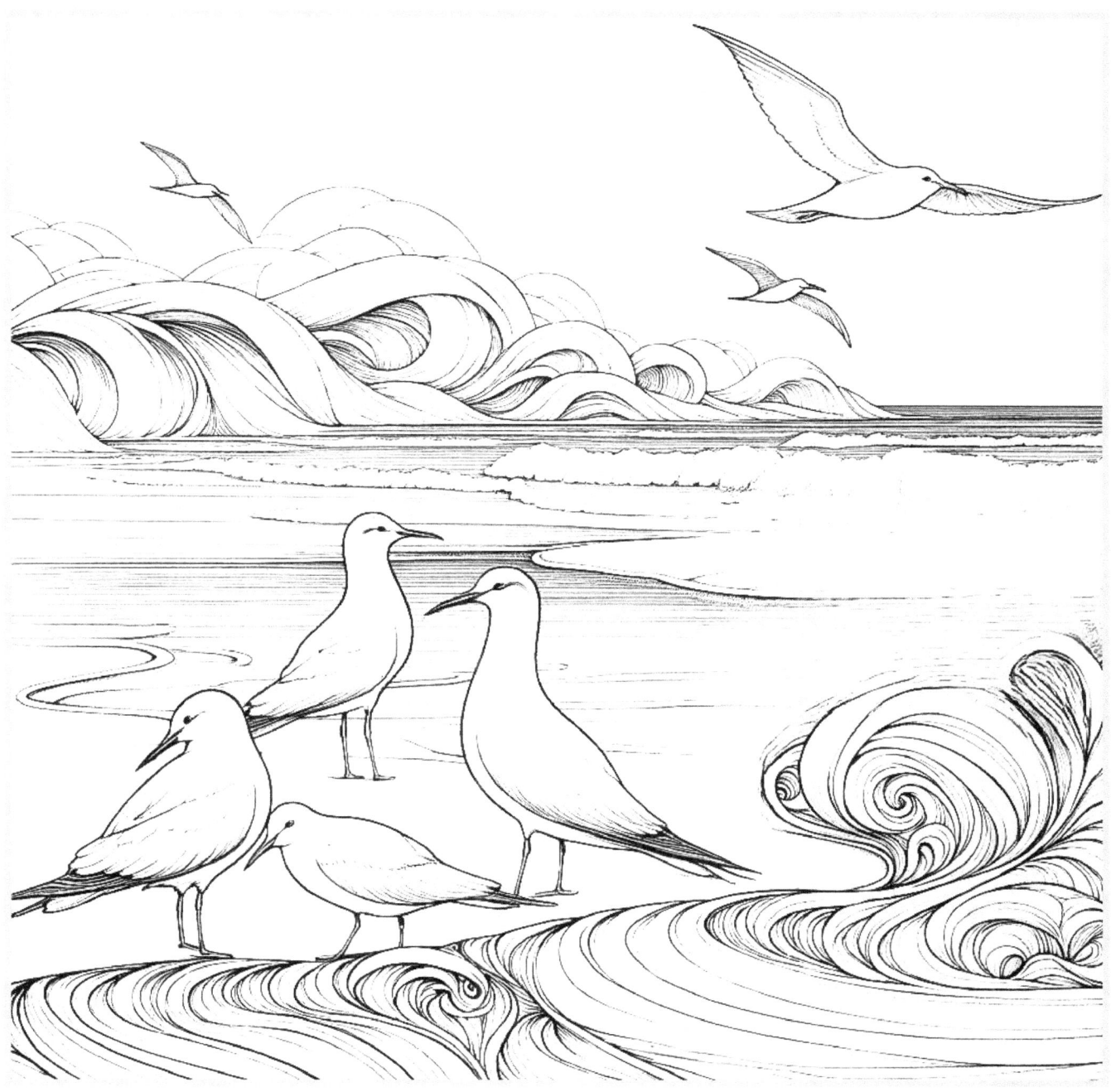

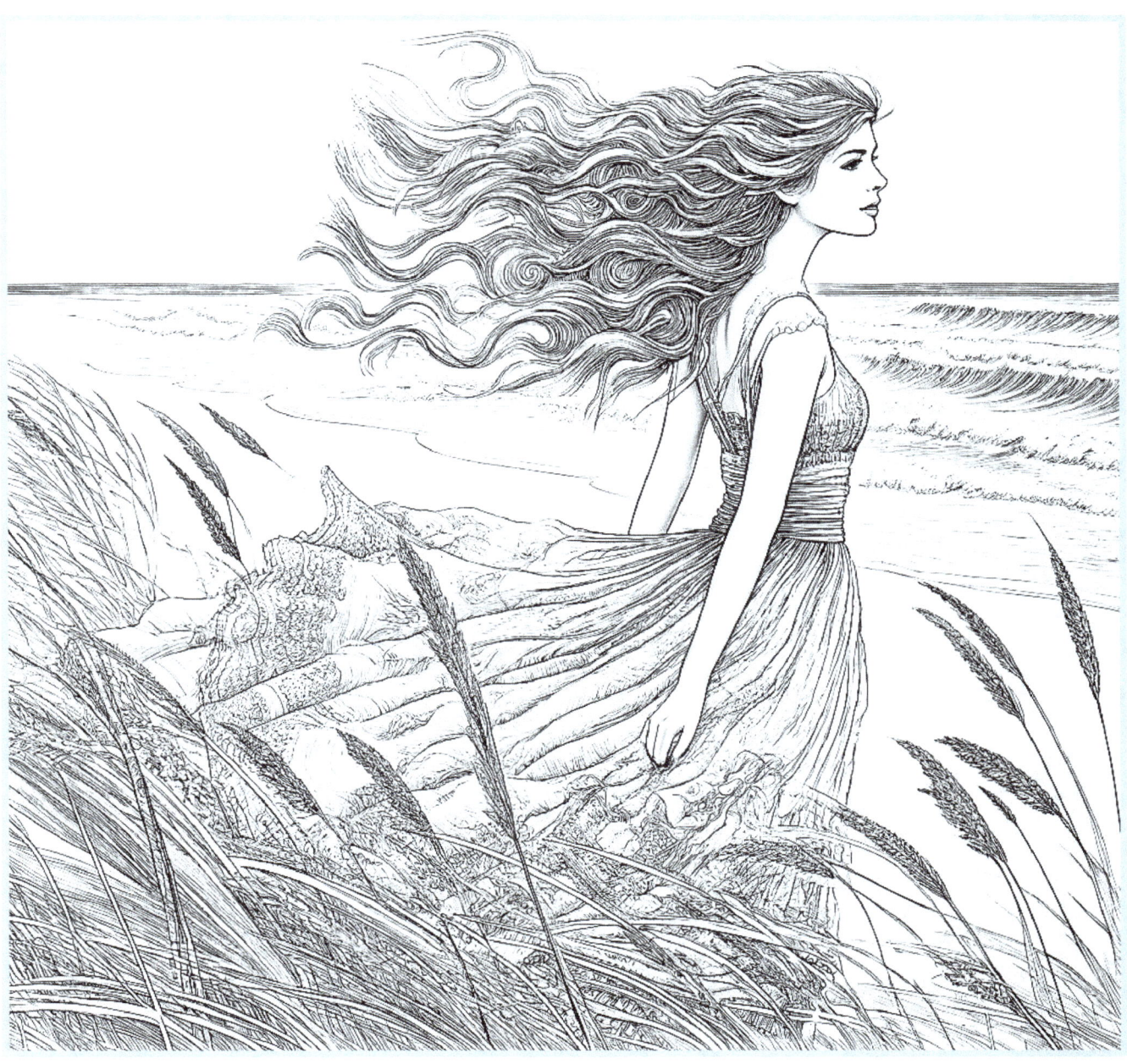

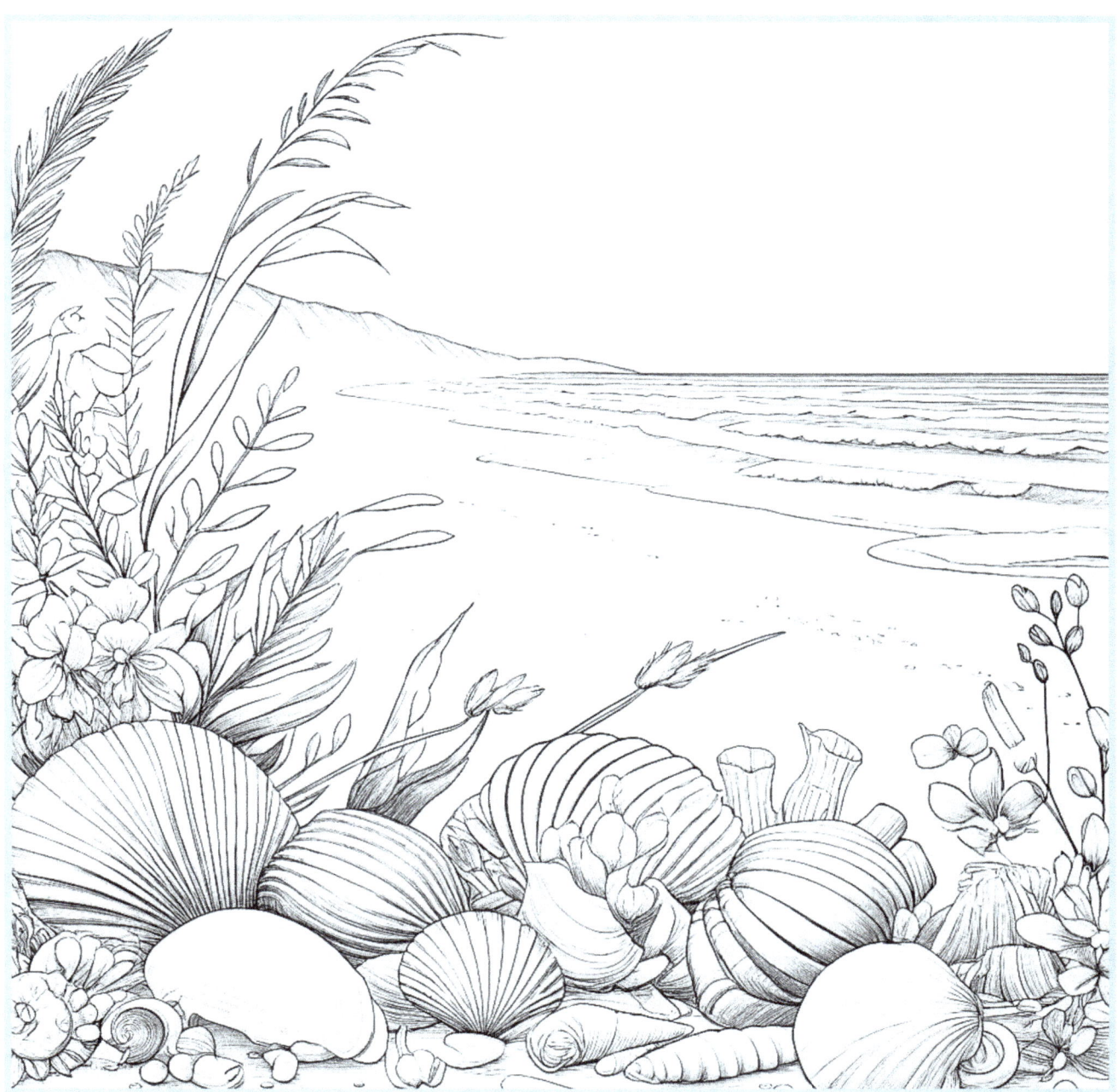

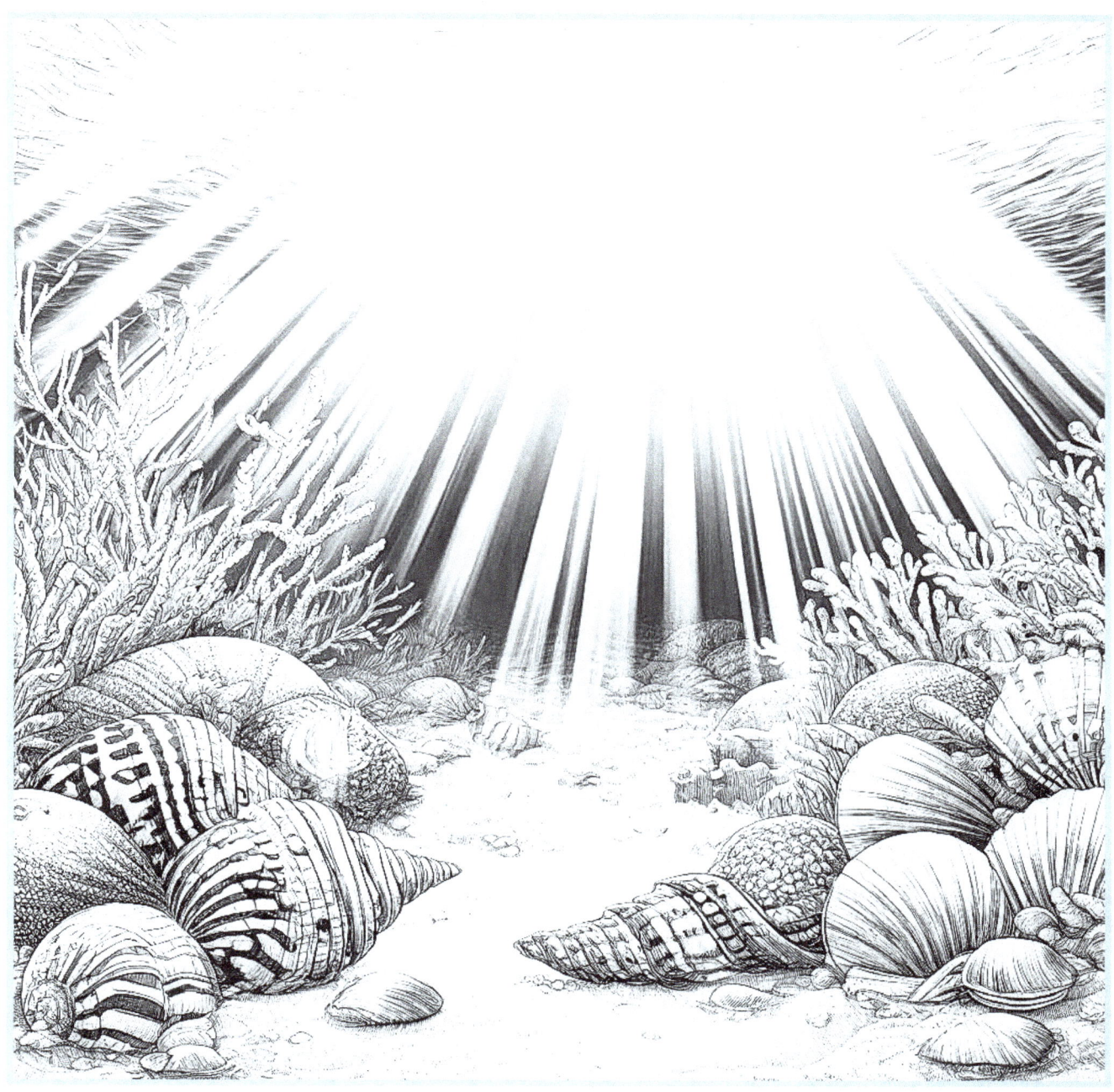

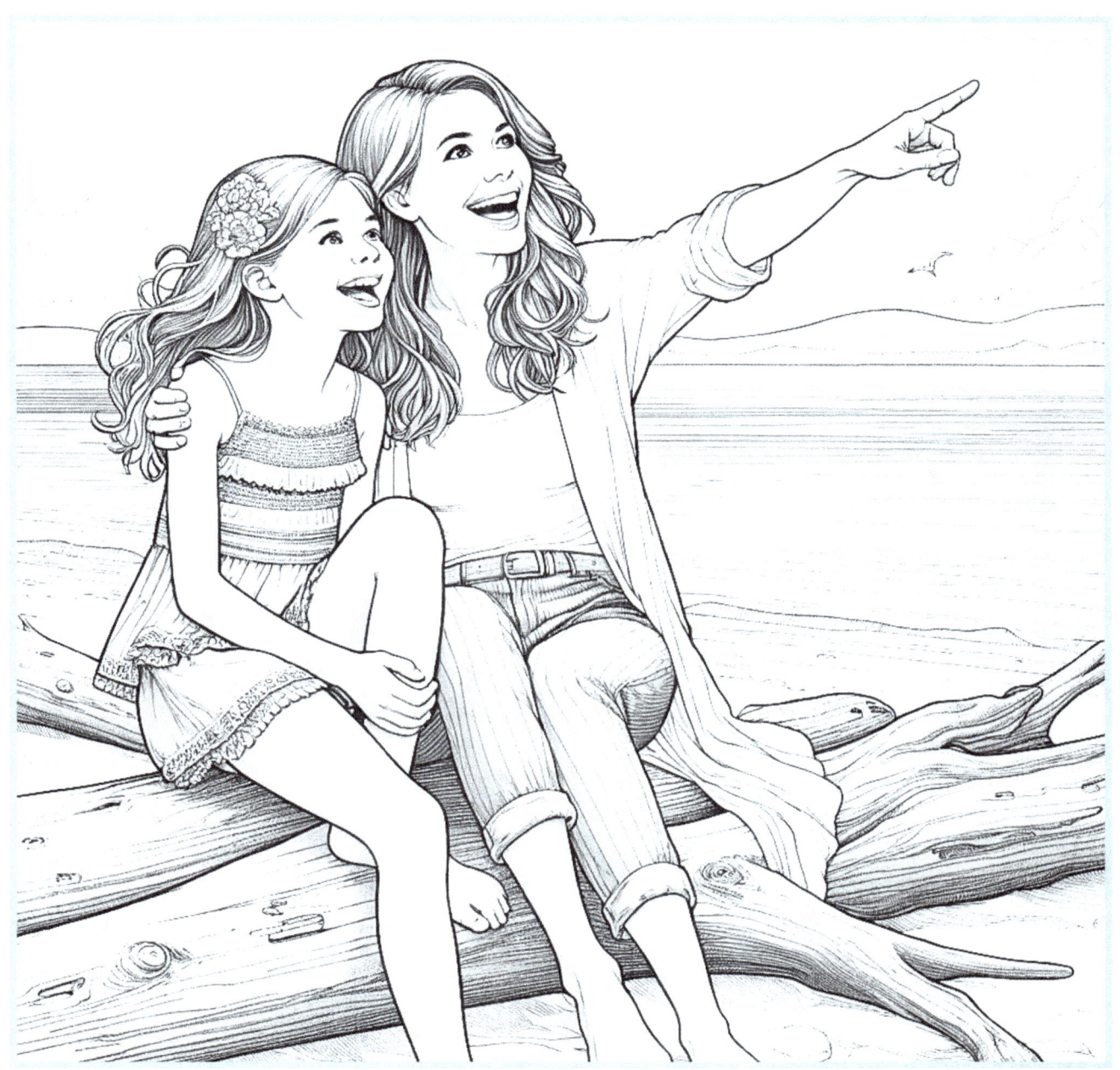

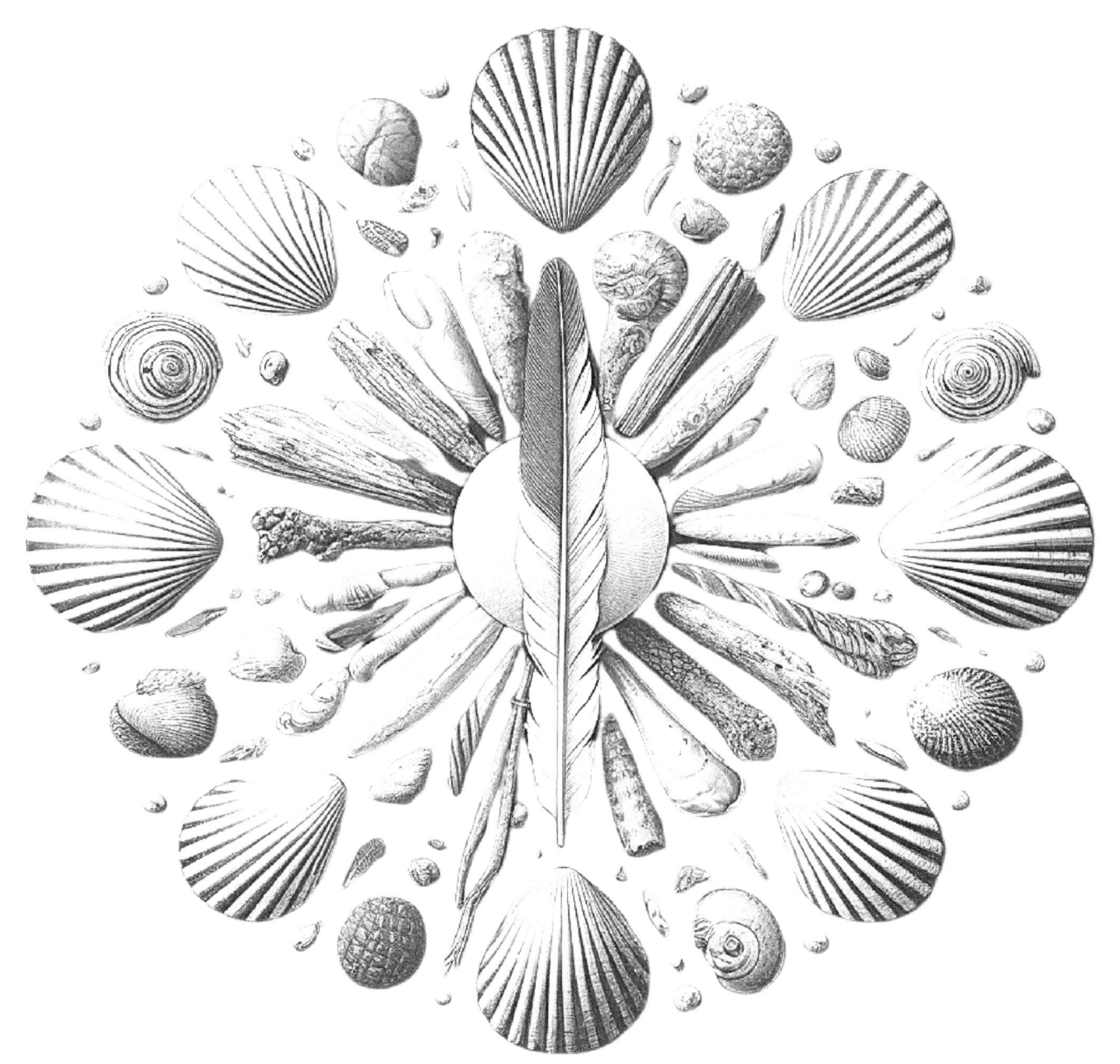

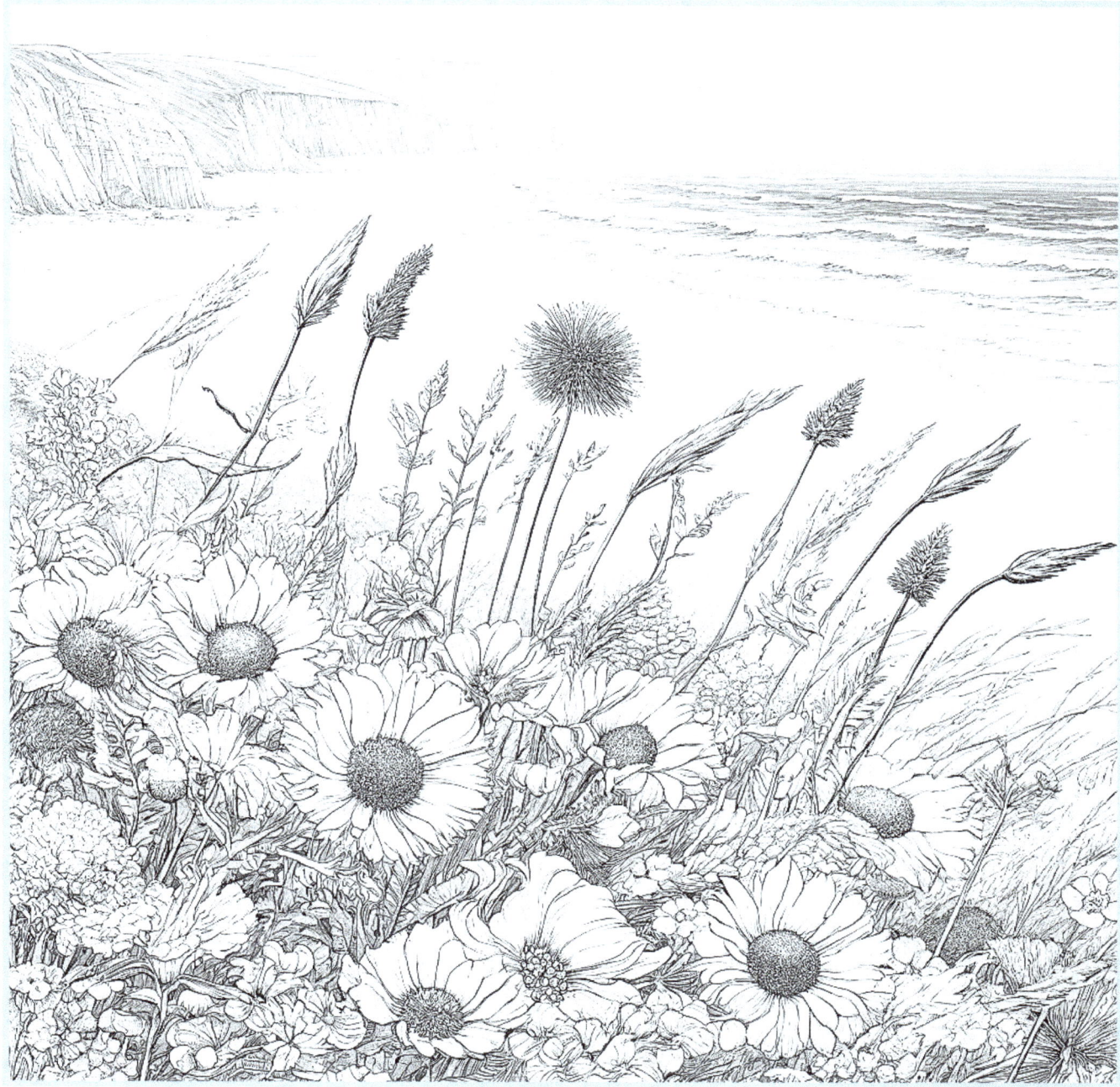

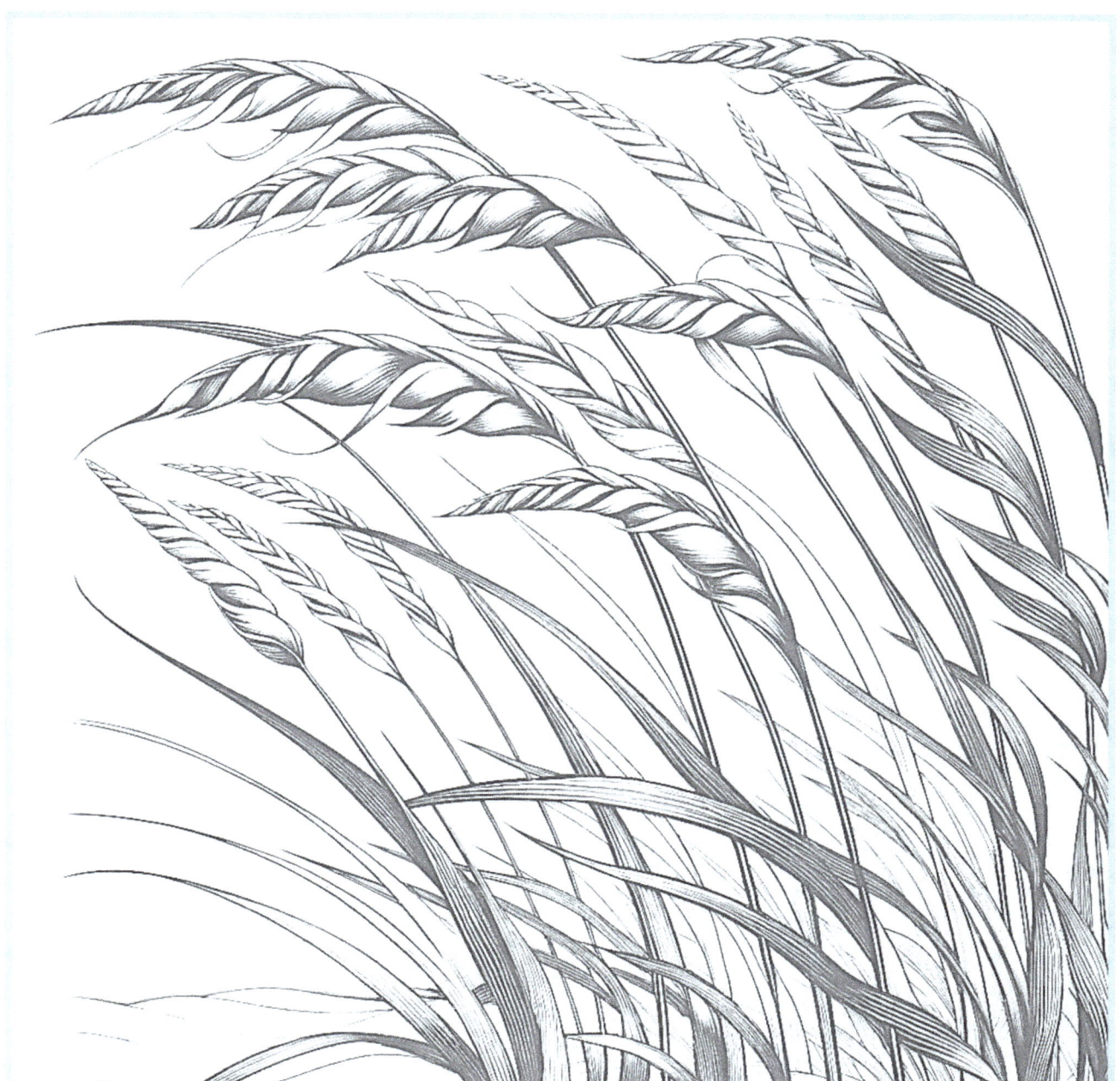

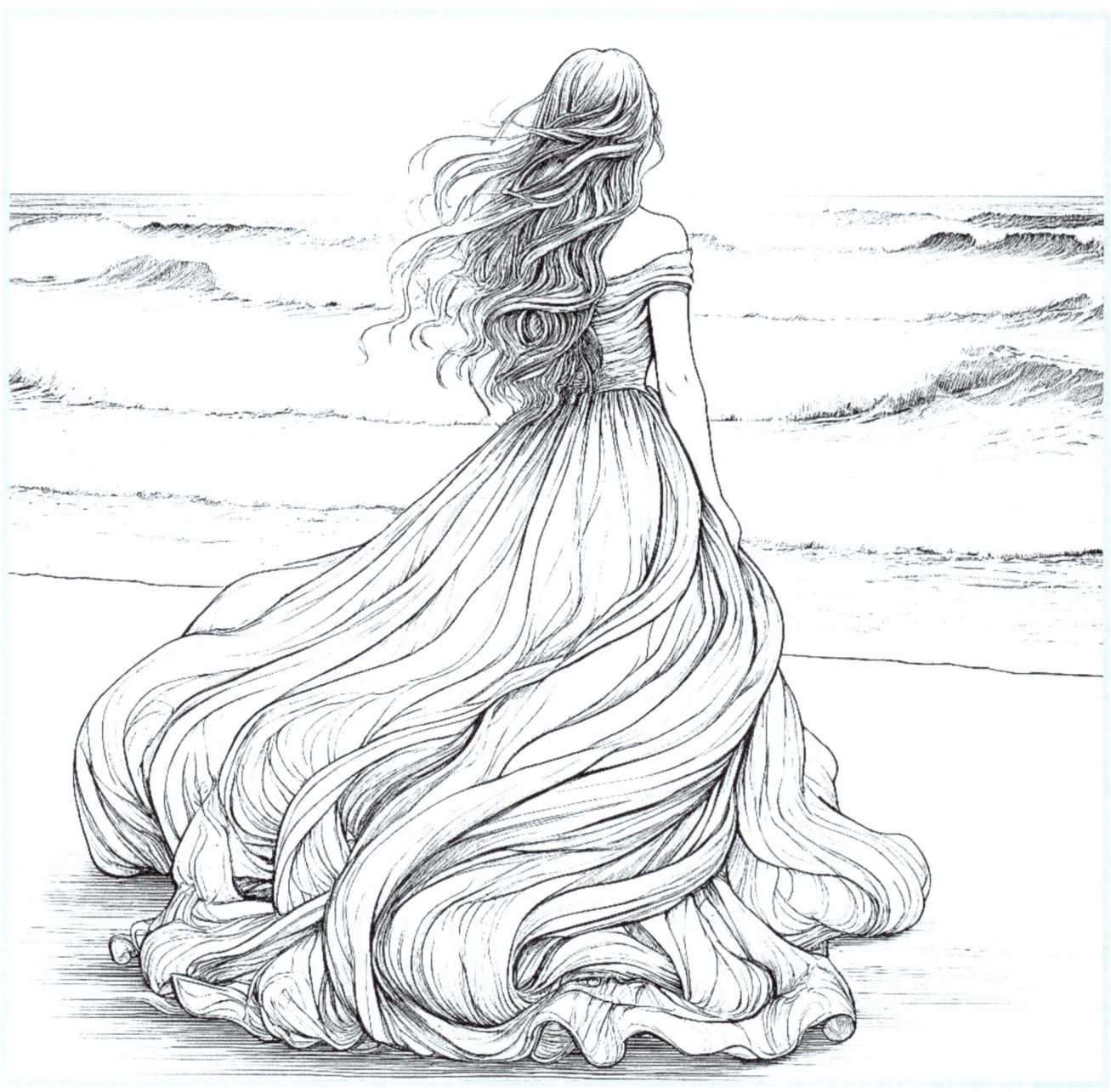

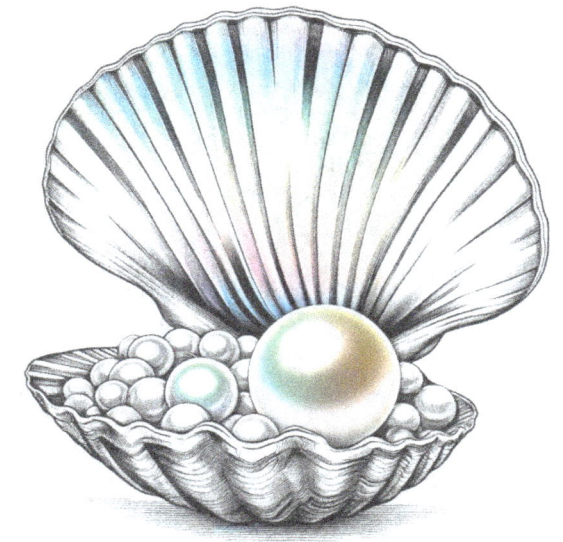

Thank you for your purchase!

Jenifer Steller

www.ingramcontent.com/pod-product-compliance
Lightning Source LLC
Chambersburg PA
CBHW062227220526
45471CB00009B/3377